Grade **3**

Scott Foresman

The Grammar & Writing Book

ISBN: 0-328-14637-4

9 10 V008 09

PEARSON

Scott
Foresman

Editorial Offices: Glenview, Illinois • Parsippany, New Jersey • New York, New York
Sales Offices: Boston, Massachusetts • Duluth, Georgia • Glenview, Illinois
Coppell, Texas • Sacramento, California • Mesa, Arizona

Table of Contents

Writer's Guide

Rubrics and Models

Evaluate Your Writing

Grammar and Writing Lessons

Writing for Tests

Grammar Patrol

Index

Writer's Guide

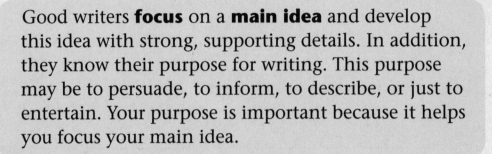

Focus/Ideas

Good writers **focus** on a **main idea** and develop this idea with strong, supporting details. In addition, they know their purpose for writing. This purpose may be to persuade, to inform, to describe, or just to entertain. Your purpose is important because it helps you focus your main idea.

A note to a friend could have this main idea and purpose:

Main Idea Convince a friend to see your new kitten

Purpose   To persuade your friend

Details give information about your main idea. Lively and interesting words make word pictures for your reader. Be sure to use only details that focus on your main idea.

- Come to see me. My kitten is fun. (no details or focus)
- Come to see my new fluffy kitten. She loves to purr and leap. (has main idea, focus, and details)

Strategies for Focus and Ideas

- Choose a topic you know well or would like to learn about. Then decide on a main idea about that topic.
- Think about your purpose for writing. An adventure story would entertain. A how-to report would inform readers.
- Look at each sentence. If it does not clearly focus on your main idea, drop it or revise it.

A Match the number of each sentence with the purpose that it fits best.

A Describe   **B** Persuade   **C** Entertain   **D** Inform

1. My dog Sandy did something funny yesterday.

2. Everyone should help clean up the park on Sunday.

3. The rainforest has more kinds of trees than any forest.

4. The shell was pearly white with ruffled edges.

B Some sentences below do not focus on the topic of the rodeo. Write the letters of those sentences.

A Two white horses danced across the ring.

B A cowboy showed how to use a lariat.

C Once I saw a white horse in a wheat field.

D A rider held on tight as a wild horse bucked.

E Cowboy clowns pretended to be afraid of a pony.

F My grandfather used to ride horses in Wyoming.

C Choose one of the main idea sentences below. Then write three sentences about the topic. Remember to use details that focus on the main idea.

- I love playing outdoors in winter.
- Cats (or dogs or hamsters) make the best pets.
- Here are three things you can do to stay healthy.

Improving Focus/Ideas

Original

Everyone has heard of the tropical rainforest. There is another kind. It is a temperate rainforest. It is like a tropical rainforest with plant life and rain, but the weather is cool.

Temperate rainforests are in Oregon and Washington. Seattle is the biggest city in Washington. Unlike the climate in the tropics, it does not rain all year in this area. The summer is dry and cool, but fog comes in with moisture.

Huge trees grow in the temperate rainforest. Some are evergreens. These trees grow where I live too. Rain and fog help the trees.

Everyone should visit the temperate rainforest.

Revising Tips

Use a strong, focused main idea statement. (Revise first paragraph to lead to this main idea sentence: Temperate rainforests have their own locations, climates, and plants.)

Use only details that focus on your main idea. (Take out *Seattle is the biggest city in Washington.*)

Use interesting words to create lively details. *(exotic birds and plants, fog rolls in, towering redwood)*

Be specific. (Tell what kind of evergreens in the third paragraph.)

Keep your purpose in mind. (Change the last sentence to reflect the informative nature of this essay.)

Improved

When you hear the word rainforest, do you think of warm temperatures and exotic birds and plants? The temperate rainforest is quite different from this. Temperate rainforests have their own locations, climates, and plants.

Temperate rainforests are found near the Pacific coast in Oregon and Washington. Unlike in tropical rainforests, it does not rain all year in this area. There is a long rainy season, but summer is dry and cool. Fog rolls in then, and brings moisture from the ocean.

Some of the hugest trees in the world grow in the temperate rainforest. These include evergreens such as the Sitka spruce and the towering redwood. Frequent rain or fog gives the rainforest trees the moisture they need to grow.

The temperate rainforest is a wet, green, beautiful corner of the world.

Writer's Corner

Use your main idea sentence like a camera lens to focus your paper. If any detail does not make the main idea clearer, remove it.

Organization/Paragraphs

A careful writer tells about events and details in order. Your **organization** builds a frame to hold your writing. The frame keeps your ideas in place.

Here are some ways to organize your writing.

- a story with a beginning, middle, and end
- a comparison-contrast
- a description from top to bottom
- a how-to explanation

Before you write your first word, think about how you will build your writing. For example, if you want to tell what happened at a school meeting, you would write a report. If you want to explain how to ride a scooter, you would write a how-to explanation.

Once you decide on your frame, choose the details you want to include. You will also have to think about how to arrange your details from beginning to end.

Strategies for Organizing Ideas

- Use a chart, story map, or web to plan out your ideas.
- Begin with the most important detail or save it for last.
- Tell events in the order they happened.
- Use order words such as *first, later,* and *last.*
- Put details that are alike in the same paragraph.

A Write the letter of the kind of organization that works best for each topic.

1. How soccer and football are alike and different

2. Instructions for making a kite

3. The treehouse in my backyard

4. A mysterious event in the school library

A Story

B How-to explanation

C Comparison-contrast

D Description

B The following details are from a paragraph that tells how to set a table. Write sentences in the correct order.

A Second, put a plate at each place.

B Then put a fork next to each napkin.

C Begin by putting placemats or a tablecloth on the table.

D Finally, put a knife and spoon to the right of the plate.

E Third, fold a napkin and put it to the left of each plate.

C Tell about a family outing or school field trip that you enjoyed. Use order words such as *first, then,* and *next* to organize the details.

Original

My family went to Grand Beach. We packed some food to take in a cooler. The adults relaxed on lounge chairs and read books. The kids built sandcastles. We used plastic buckets to find sea animals in the shallow water. Before that, though, we found a good place to put our blanket, umbrella, and chairs. Everyone took a long walk on the beach. At lunchtime we had a picnic under the umbrella. Mom joined us swimming. My parents, brother, aunt, uncle, and cousin all squeezed into the van. The sun started to go down, and we packed up everything and left.

Revising Tips

Give important facts at the beginning. (The second-to-the-last sentence tells who went to the beach and sets the day in motion. It should be put close to the beginning.)

Use an order that makes sense. Tell events in the order they happen. (Move up information in the sixth sentence.)

Use order words to help your reader understand what happened. (Add words and phrases such as *then, next,* and *after a short rest.*)

Start a new paragraph when the topic shifts. (Put the afternoon events in a second paragraph.)

Write a conclusion to tie details together. (*We were tired but happy after a long day at the beach* sums up the day.)

Improved

Last summer my family went to Grand Beach. My parents, brother, aunt, uncle, and cousin all squeezed into the van. We packed sandwiches, fruit, and juice in a cooler. When we arrived, we found a good place to put our blanket, umbrella, and chairs. Next, everyone took a long walk on the beach. Then the adults relaxed on lounge chairs and read books while the kids built sandcastles. We also used plastic buckets to find sea animals in the shallow water.

At lunchtime we had a picnic under the umbrella. After a short rest, Mom joined us swimming. When the sun started to go down, we packed up everything and left. We were tired but happy after a long day at the beach.

Writer's Corner

Although you won't actually say "the end" after your last written word, readers should know you have finished. A good conclusion (whether it's a question for readers, a summarizing sentence, or an echo of the beginning) makes your writing complete.

Voice

Your writing shows your special style and personality. Use your writer's **voice** to shape your writing. A writer's voice may be funny or serious. It could be friendly or formal. When your writing voice is strong and clear, readers believe what you have to say.

- I was so tired that I got into bed early. (weak voice)
- I was so worn out that I crawled into bed an hour before dinnertime. I didn't wake up until Dad shouted that breakfast was ready. (strong voice)

Strategies for Developing a Writer's Voice

- Think about your readers and about your reason for writing. Use a light, friendly voice when you write a letter to a cousin or when you tell a funny story. Use a more serious voice for a book report or for directions.
- Your choice of words should match your voice. In informal writing, you might use contractions or slang to make your writing sound like your everyday voice. A letter to the editor of your school newspaper would have a more serious voice.
- Use your writer's voice to speak directly to your audience. If your voice is strong, readers will want to keep on reading.
- Different types of sentences add to voice. Engage readers by asking a question or giving a command.

A Match each opening sentence with the letter of the reader it fits best.

A Your cousin Jenny in Hawaii

B The editor of a town newspaper

C Your teacher and classmates

D Kids in your neighborhood

1. I believe that everyone in town should support the clean-up project organized by our school.

2. Let's plan the greatest block party ever!

3. You won't believe what happened here last weekend!

4. Marsupials are a fascinating group of animals.

B Match each kind of voice with the writing it would fit best.

A funny   **B** persuasive   **C** serious   **D** friendly

5. an invitation asking students to attend the class play

6. a letter trying to convince people to come to a school bake sale

7. an article about a recent hurricane

8. a story about a talking cow

C Choose one of the following opening sentences. Add sentences to write a paragraph about the topic. Use a voice that fits your main idea and audience.

- If your brothers and sisters drive you nuts, here are some tips for getting along with them.

- You're never too young to help people in your community.

Improving Voice

Original

Dear Editor,

    Our school district said we might not get to take music classes during the school day from now on. This isn't fair! I love singing and learning to play an instrument. Besides, Toby, Alex, and I have a really cool time writing our own songs and singing them together. I guess we would be able to take music on our own after school. But this wouldn't be the same. Everyone wouldn't get to take extra classes, and I would miss my friends. I might also have to stop playing soccer to take music. Don't be so unfair! Don't take our music away from us!

Revising Tips

Keep your audience and purpose in mind. (Readers of letters to the editor do not know you, Toby, or Alex. Use examples that appeal to a wider audience, such as *Many students have other after-school activities*.)

Use appropriate words. (Replace words such as *cool* and contractions such as *wouldn't*. Appropriate modifiers such as *happy* and *well-rounded* strengthen your argument.)

Choose a strong but pleasant voice. (*This isn't fair* makes you sound negative instead of responsible and logical.)

Improved

Dear Editor,

    Our school district said we might not get to take music classes during the school day from now on. This would be a shame. Right now all students can sing and learn to play an instrument in our school's music classes. Music is very different from math and spelling, but it is just as important. In our music classes, students learn new skills and get to be creative. Also, we really enjoy ourselves. It is fun to sing and play music together.

    If music classes are canceled, students would be able to sign up for special music classes after school. Yet everyone would not be able to take extra classes. Many students have other after-school activities such as sports that would conflict with music classes. Learning music makes us happy and well-rounded. Parents and children should try to save music in our schools.

Writer's Corner

Is the voice in your writing the real you? Is it a person people will trust and enjoy listening to? Try reading your work aloud to answer these questions.

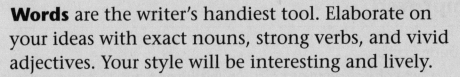

Word Choice

Words are the writer's handiest tool. Elaborate on your ideas with exact nouns, strong verbs, and vivid adjectives. Your style will be interesting and lively.

- I like the bakery because it smells good. (dull and plain)
- The bakery smells like sweet cinnamon rolls and fresh, crusty bread. (lively and detailed)

Strategies for Choosing the Right Words

- Choose exact nouns. (*spaniel* instead of dog, *broccoli* instead of *vegetable*)
- Use strong verbs. (*shatter* instead of *break, shriek* instead of *yell*)
- Replace dull words such as *nice, bad,* and *thing* with clear words. ("The owner was greedy and cruel" instead of "The owner was bad.")
- Include words that use our senses. ("The sun was as warm as a blanket" instead of "The sun was warm.")
- Don't be wordy. (*happily* instead of "with great happiness")
- Elaborate with specific details. ("Dan slurped up soup and ate crackers" instead of "Dan was a noisy eater.")

A Replace the underlined words with more exact words from the box. Write the paragraph.

| climbs | shrubs and wildflowers |
| observes | brisk | wanders |

(1) Each weekend Luis takes a <u>nice</u> hike. (2) He <u>walks</u> up steep hills. (3) The path <u>goes</u> through the forest. (4) He often <u>sees</u> amazing birds and animals. (5) The <u>plants</u> always surprise him.

B Change each underlined word to a more vivid word of your own. Write the sentences.

6. Luis and Jackie rode horses through a green <u>place</u>.
7. The horses had <u>nice</u> coats.
8. They came to a fence that was <u>big</u>.
9. Luis's horse <u>went</u> over the fence.
10. Jackie's horse stood on the <u>ground</u>.
11. Jackie <u>talked</u> to the horse.
12. The horse seemed <u>upset</u>.

C Write a description of a certain kind or quality of weather, such as a snowstorm, thunderstorm, wind, or bright sunshine. Use exact nouns, strong verbs, and vivid adjectives.

Improving Word Choice

Original

Our city has many hills. These hills are of many sizes because some are big and some are not so big. From the top of them you can see the bridge that goes across the river. You can see all the city's big buildings. Cars go slowly up the hills and then go down. Other vehicles have a hard time getting up the hills. People also have a hard time as they walk up the hills. They have to work hard as they go down the hills too, or they would go too fast. Our city's hills are hard to climb.

Revising Tips

Replace vague nouns with precise ones. (Replace *big buildings* with *skyscrapers*. Replace *other vehicles* with *buses and trucks*.)

Replace weak verbs with strong ones. (Use *creep* and *struggle* instead of *go*. Use *trudge* and *shuffle* instead of *walk*.)

Elaborate with words that help readers see, hear, taste, smell, and feel what you are describing. (*glass and concrete skyscrapers, people huff and puff, plunge*)

Replace dull adjectives with vivid ones. (Use *sky-high* instead of *big, challenging* instead of *hard*.)

Avoid wordiness. Rewrite sentences that contain unnecessary words. (Shorten and refocus the second sentence.)

Improved

Our city has many hills. Some seem sky-high, while others rise gently above the streets and avenues. From the top of the highest hills you can see the old-fashioned bridge that spans the river. You can see all the city's glass and concrete skyscrapers. Cars creep up the hills and then fly down. Buses and trucks struggle up the hills. People huff and puff as they trudge up the hills. They slant backwards as they shuffle down, using their feet as brakes so they don't plunge headlong down the slope. Our city's hills are challenging, but the city wouldn't be the same without them.

Writer's Corner

Use as few words as possible to express your ideas. For example, you can say a bridge *spans* a river instead of *goes across* it. Choices such as these will make your writing stronger.

Sentences

Good writing has a natural flow. Different kinds of **sentences** should make it sound smooth and clear. When you hear a story read aloud, listen to the style and the rhythm of the sentences.

Here are some ways to improve your sentences.

- Use different kinds of sentences. Questions, commands, and exclamations add style to your writing.
- Make sure your sentences are not all short and choppy. Sometimes a longer sentence helps the writing flow.
- Use different beginnings. Starting too many sentences with *I, she, the,* or *a* can be boring.
- Use connecting words. Words such as *even though, because, while,* and *but* can join sentences and show how ideas are related.
- Don't write long, stringy sentences. Too many sentences combined with *and* or *so* make your reader lose interest.

Strategy for Improving Your Sentences

Read a piece of your writing.

- Each time you start a sentence with *I, she, the,* or *a,* circle the word.
- Underline all the short, choppy sentences.
- See how many different kinds of sentences you use. Then revise these sentences to make your writing better.

A Use the connecting words in ( ) to join the two sentences. Write the sentences.

> **Example:**   Spot barked. He saw his food. (When)
> **Answer:**   Spot barked when he saw his food.

   1. Chad wanted to bowl. He had never tried it before. (even though)

   2. Mrs. Jackson read a book. Sophie went to dance class. (while)

   3. The Taylors went to a fancy restaurant. It was Joey's birthday. (because)

   4. Tony put on comfortable shoes. His feet still hurt. (but)

B Rearrange the words in sentences 5–8 so that A is not the first word. Start with the underlined phrase.

> **Example:**   I ate a big lunch <u>today</u>.
> **Answer:**   Today I ate a big lunch.

   The night was calm and peaceful. **(5)** A big orange moon glowed brightly <u>above the mountains</u>. **(6)** A gentle wind rustled the leaves <u>in the forest</u>. **(7)** A bird began singing <u>just before sunrise</u>. **(8)** A new day was beginning <u>once again</u>.

C Write a story about a person and an animal who are friends. Use different kinds of sentences. Be sure to begin your sentences with different words.

Improving Sentences

Original

My sister Renata is generous. She is just a teenager. She always finds ways to help others. She organized a coat drive. People donated old coats. She gave them to people in need. She heard about an earthquake in Asia, so she collected money from the students in her school, and she sent more than $500 to the earthquake survivors. Renata does other helpful things. She works at a homeless shelter. She visits senior citizens who live in a special home. Renata is always thinking about others. She is my role model.

Revising Tips

Use different beginnings. Don't start all sentences with the subject. (Reword some sentences that begin with *She*.)

Join choppy sentences with connecting words that show how ideas are related. (*Although she is just a teenager, she always finds ways to help others* instead of *She is just a teenager. She always finds ways to help others.*)

Rewrite long, stringy sentences. Use stronger connecting words, and break some sentences into two. (*When Renata heard about an earthquake in Asia, she collected money from the students in her school.*)

Vary kinds and lengths of sentences. Use questions, exclamations, and commands as well as statements.

Improved

What makes a person truly generous? Listen to some things that my sister Renata does. Although she is just a teenager, she always finds ways to help others. For example, she organized a coat drive. People donated old coats, and Renata gave them to people in need. When Renata heard about an earthquake in Asia, she collected money from the students in her school. She sent more than $500 to the earthquake survivors. Renata does other helpful things as well. She works at a homeless shelter and visits senior citizens who live in a special home. Renata is always thinking about others. Is it any wonder she is my role model?

Writer's Corner

Try using a question, command, or exclamation as an introduction or conclusion. These kinds of sentences will get your readers' attention.

Conventions

Conventions are rules for writing. Capital letters show where a sentence begins. A period, question mark, or exclamation mark signals the end of a sentence. A new paragraph begins with an indentation. Grammar and spelling follow patterns.

- joe asted his techur for a pensul then he could gets to work. (weak conventions)
- Joe asked his teacher for a pencil. Then he could get to work. (strong conventions)

Strategies for Conventions of Writing

- Start sentences with a capital letter and end with the proper punctuation mark.
- Make sure each sentence tells a complete idea. Each subject and verb should agree.
- Use the correct forms of verbs.
- Capitalize all important words in proper nouns.
- Follow rules for punctuation marks.
- Use pronouns and modifiers correctly.
- Use a dictionary or spell checker for difficult words.

Proofreading Marks

¶ New paragraph

≡ Capital letter

/ Lowercase letter

○ Correct the spelling.

∧ Add something.

⌒ Remove something.

A Choose the correct word in ( ) to complete each sentence. Write the sentences.

> **1.** My parents and (I, me) rode a train across country.
>
> **2.** We have (saw, seen) many beautiful sights.
>
> **3.** Trains (takes, take) much longer than airplanes.
>
> **4.** You (learning, learn) about the country on a train.
>
> **5.** The train was fun for me and (they, them).

B Look at each sentence. Correct any mistakes in punctuation, grammar, and spelling. Write the paragraph.

> **(6)** Last summer melinda went to hawaii. **(7)** Did she right you a postcard. **(8)** The blue ocean and white sand makes the islands beutiful. **(9)** rainforests beaches and mountains attract many tourists. **(10)** Dont you want to visit our 50th state.

C Write three sentences about one of the topics below. Follow the rules for capitalization, punctuation, grammar, and spelling. Trade papers with a classmate and look for anything that should be changed.

- A hiking or camping trip I took
- My favorite holiday
- Something I collect

Improving Conventions

Original

I have went to many museums. I even have been to a natural history museum to see Dinosaurs. But my favrit museum is the Air and Space Museum in washington. This museum has evrything about flying. It have gliders airplanes and rockets. There is a big exhibit about Wilbur and orville Wright. You can even see the first airplane they flew. The museum has the plane that Charles Lindbergh flown across the ocean in 1927 as well as some of the earlyest spaceships. My sister and me spent hour's at this museum and didnt get tired. Does flying interest you. Then go the Air and Space Museum!

Revising Tips

Check for correct capitalization of sentences and of proper nouns. *(Dinosaurs, washington, orville)*

Look for misspellings. *(favrit, everythin, earlyest)*

Make sure you have used punctuation, including apostrophes, correctly. *(hour's, didnt, interest you)*

Check for correct pronoun usage. *(My sister and me spent)*

Check for correct verb forms. *(I have went, Charles Lindbergh flown)*

Make sure that subjects and verbs agree. *(It have)*

Improved

I have gone to many museums. I have even been to a natural history museum to see dinosaurs. But my favorite museum is the Air and Space Museum in Washington. This museum has everything about flying. It has gliders, airplanes, and rockets. There is a big exhibit about Wilbur and Orville Wright. You can even see the first airplane they flew. The museum has the plane that Charles Lindbergh flew across the Atlantic in 1927 as well as some of the earliest spaceships. My sister and I spent hours at this museum and didn't get tired. Does flying interest you? Then go the Air and Space Museum!

Writer's Corner

Sometimes it's hard to catch your own mistakes. Use a ruler to check each line of your paper from start to finish. If you're trying to focus on spelling errors, read your sentences backwards. That way you won't be distracted by their meaning.

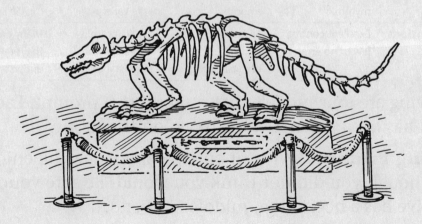

Rubrics and Models

Narrative Writing *Scoring Rubric*

A scoring **rubric** can be used to judge a piece of writing. A rubric is a checklist of traits, or writing skills, to look for. See pages 2–25 for a discussion of these traits. Rubrics give a number score for each trait.

Score	4	3	2	1
Focus/Ideas	Excellent narrative focused on a clear main idea; strong elaboration	Good narrative mostly focused on a main idea; good elaboration	Unfocused narrative with unrelated details; little elaboration	Rambling narrative with unrelated details
Organization/ Paragraphs	Strong beginning, middle, and end, with appropriate order words	Adequate beginning, middle, and end, with some order words	Little direction from beginning to end, with few order words	Lacks beginning, middle, end, with incorrect or no order words
Voice	Writer involved— personality evident	Reveals personality at times	Little writer involvement	Careless writing with no feeling
Word Choice	Vivid, precise words that bring story to life	Adequate words that bring story to life	Few vivid or interesting words	Vague, dull, or misused words
Sentences	Excellent variety of sentences; natural rhythm	Varied lengths, styles, generally smooth	Simple, awkward, or wordy sentences; little variety	Choppy, many incomplete or run-on sentences
Conventions	Excellent control; few or no errors	No serious errors to affect understanding	Weak control; errors affect understanding	Many errors that prevent understanding

Following are four models that respond to a prompt. Each model has been given a score, based on the rubric.

Writing Prompt   Write about an experience you enjoyed even though you did not think you would. Be sure your narrative has a beginning, middle, and end.

Narrative Writing Model *Score 4*

Did you ever want to go to the bottom of the ocean? Well, I didn't! Last summer my family visited my grandma in Florida. One day my dad said, "Today we're going snorkeling!" I was excited. Then I found out I would have a mask over my face. I would breathe through a little tube. Snorkelers don't go deep, so the tube sticks up into the air.

I didn't like the idea of breathing underwater. Even though I was nervous, I went to the beach. The water was crystal clear. My dad took his time and helped me use the snorkel. I stayed underwater for longer and longer. The fishes and plants were amazing rainbows of color. Now I can't wait to go snorkeling in Florida again.

Focus/Ideas Focused on the snorkeling experience; supported with details

Organization/Paragraphs Events in order and broken into paragraphs; connecting words *(one day, then, now)* that move story along

Voice Expresses unique personality *(Well, I didn't!)*

Word Choice Precise word choice and vivid imagery *(mask over my face, little tube, crystal clear, rainbows of color)*

Sentences Variety of sentence kinds and lengths

Conventions No errors

Narrative Writing Model *Score 3*

My mom talked me into joining the soccer team. She said that I always liked to run and kick and let off steam. But I just like to play with my friends in the neigborhood. Not on a real team. We have fun kicking the ball around on the playground. I knew that I would have practice twice a week and a game once a week. Who's got time for that? Anyway, I started going to practices and games, and they turned out to be fun. Now I like soccer alot. I've learned teamwork and strategies. My team has won some games, and I feel I've contributed.

Focus/Ideas   Main idea of not wanting to join soccer team clear and most details focused on that experience

Organization/Paragraphs   Beginning and end clear; could use more connecting words

Voice   Writer's feelings and change revealed in the last three sentences and in *Who's got time for that?*

Word Choice   Some precise words *(teamwork, strategies)*; some dull words *(fun)*

Sentences   Variety (complex and compound sentences)

Conventions   Sentence fragment *(Not on a real team)*; some spelling errors *(neigborhood, alot)*

Narrative Writing Model *Score 2*

The main thing I didn't want to do was go to my swimming lessons because the water was always cold and the teacher made us do excersises and praktis the hole time. I had hard time learning to tread water so the teacher made me keep praktis even thogh I got tired. Well now I can swim and I can also tread water, so I guess its a good thing I took lessons.

Focus/Ideas   Focused on the experience with several supporting details

Organization/Paragraphs   Moves from a beginning to an end; needs introduction that engages reader

Voice   Gives readers a sense of who the writer is

Word Choice   Limited, dull word choice (*do, got*)

Sentences   Wordy and strung together with many *and's* and other connectors

Conventions   Many misspellings; omitted words (*I had hard time*); wording errors (*made me keep praktis*), no paragraph indent

Narrative Writing Model *Score 1*

> I didn want go to the party but my mom said I shod so I put on my favrite swettr. Because I just move in the nabor hood and didn no anyone. So I go Everyone was nice and fun and mad the gam the party was fun too. So my frends and me gong to partys if they invite me.

Focus/Ideas   Unclear description of the party

Organization/Paragraphs   Events in sequence but need connecting words

Voice   Errors detract from sense of writer's personality

Word Choice   Limited, dull word choice *(nice, fun)*

Sentences   Long, stringy sentences; overuse of *and, so*

Conventions   Many errors that interfere with meaning

Descriptive Writing *Scoring Rubric*

Score	4	3	2	1
Focus/Ideas	Excellent description with clear main idea and strong, elaborated details	Good description with adequate details focused on main idea	Some descriptive details; some focus on main idea	Little focus on described subject; lacks details
Organization/ Paragraphs	Details arranged in clear order; strong beginning and ending	Details mostly arranged in order; good beginning and ending	Details not well connected; poor beginning and ending	No organization to details; lack of beginning or ending
Voice	Strong personality; clear connection between writer and subject	Writer involved; some connection between writer and subject	Writer lacking involvement; few feelings shown	Writer involvement, point of view missing
Word Choice	Specific, vivid language that appeals to several senses	Accurate, engaging language that appeals to one or two senses	Uninteresting language; little appeal to senses	Limited, vague language; repetitive
Sentences	Superior structure; excellent flow	Some varied beginnings; well constructed	Simple structures; little variety	Many errors; awkward, hard to read
Conventions	Excellent control; few or no errors	No serious errors to affect understanding	Weak control; enough errors to affect understanding	Many errors that prevent understanding

Following are four models that respond to a prompt. Each model has been given a score, based on the rubric.

Writing Prompt   Describe your favorite animal. It may be a pet that you know well or a wild animal that you have read about. Use exact words to help readers see, hear, taste, smell, and feel what you are describing.

Descriptive Writing Model *Score 4*

My cocker spaniel Sadie has blond curly fur and big brown eyes. She has a soft bark and a tongue that feels like sandpaper. Sadie has many ways to let me know how she feels.

Sadie shows some feelings with her face. Sometimes she tilts her head as if she is wondering about something. Sometimes her eyes and mouth look like she is smiling.

The rest of Sadie's body shows feelings too. When she is excited, her tail moves back and forth like a swing at the playground. Her claws make happy little clattering sounds as she runs across the kitchen to greet me.

I guess I am playing favorites, but I think Sadie is the most beautiful and intelligent dog in the world.

Focus/Ideas   Strong focus with many supporting details

Organization/Paragraphs   Engaging introduction, conclusion, and body paragraphs

Voice   Clearly communicates feelings for pet

Word Choice   Vivid word choice and images that appeal to touch, sight, and hearing (*a tongue that feels like sandpaper, like a swing at the playground, little clattering sounds*)

Sentences   Clear sentences of various kinds and lengths

Conventions   No errors

Descriptive Writing Model *Score 3*

I think tigers are so interesting. First of all, they are beautiful they have unusul coats, usully with orange and black stripes. They also have big round heads and long whiskers. They are big but they are very graceful. They move very smoothly, as if they are gliding across the ground.

Tigers are scary when they roar very loud. You can still tell they are related to cute little kitty cats that run around the neighborhood. I think tigers are the most beautiful and interesting animals we have.

Focus/Ideas Focused on qualities of tigers and supported with many details

Organization/Paragraphs A few transitions *(First of all, also)*; needs better introduction and conclusion

Voice Writer's appreciation of tigers communicated

Word Choice Some vivid words *(graceful)*; phrases that appeal to sight *(as if they are gliding across the ground)*; some overused modifiers *(beautiful, big, cute)*

Sentences Variety in kind and length; many sentences beginning with *They*

Conventions A run-on sentence; spelling errors *(unusul, usully)*

Descriptive Writing Model *Score 2*

> Whales are so cool they are huge and live in the water but yet they consider them mammals. A whale has black shinny skin and it dive deep in the water. Then it comes back to the top agin and blows water throgh it's spout. A whale has a funny tail that has two points and sometimes it stiks it's tail out of the water only. Some whales are smaller and don't have black skin.

Focus/Ideas   Focused on the subject, some descriptive details

Organization/Paragraphs   Some organization evident but not consistent; needs clear conclusion

Voice   Shows enthusiasm for topic

Word Choice   Some vivid words appealing to sight and sound; some vague or dull words *(cool, funny)*

Sentences   Run-on at beginning; other sentences are grammatical but have little variety

Conventions   Many misspellings; vague pronoun references *(they consider them mammals)*; errors in subject-verb agreement *(it dive)*

Descriptive Writing Model *Score 1*

My cats cute. With long fur. He is fluffy and he has a long tail and he has wite spots on his stomik. He has wite paws too and you cant hear him. He comes into the room. He meow sometimes but he dont like most peeple only the ones that take care of.

Focus/Ideas   Attempts specific descriptions but loses focus with details on cat's relationship with people

Organization/Paragraphs   Descriptions in no logical order; no ending

Voice   Little voice evident

Word Choice   Limited word choice; some appeal to sight and sound

Sentences   Overuse of the connecting word *and*; many sentences beginning with *He*

Conventions   A fragment; omission of apostrophes for contractions; many misspellings; errors in subject-verb agreement *(he meow, he dont)*

Persuasive Writing *Scoring Rubric*

Score	4	3	2	1
Focus/Ideas	Excellent persuasive essay with clearly stated opinion and strong elaboration	Clear opinion supported by mostly persuasive reasons	Opinion not clearly stated, weak reasons or not enough support	No stated opinion, details not focused on topic
Organization/ Paragraphs	Strong, convincing introduction; reasons presented in order of importance	Interesting introduction; reasons in order of importance	Weak or unclear introduction; reasons not clear or not in order of importance	No introduction; few reasons; order not logical
Voice	Concerned, committed writer behind words	Some sense of caring; concerned writer behind words	Little sense of writer involvement	No sense of writer's personality or feelings evident
Word Choice	Effective use of persuasive words	Use of persuasive words adequate to good	Few persuasive words used in essay	No persuasive words used in essay
Sentences	Varied sentence structures; excellent flow and rhythm	Some varied sentence structures; few sentence errors	Limited to simple sentences; some errors	Simple, choppy sentences; fragments and run-ons
Conventions	Excellent control of all mechanical aspects of writing	Few errors in grammar, spelling, punctuation, paragraphing	Some distracting mechanical errors	Many errors that prevent understanding

Following are four models that respond to a prompt. Each model has been given a score, based on the rubric.

Writing Prompt   Think about a new activity or some other change that would improve your school. Write a letter to your principal. Try to persuade him or her to make the change by giving several good reasons for it.

Persuasive Writing Model *Score 4*

Dear Mr. Henry,

    I think we should start a school orchestra. First of all, many students take music lessons and could join. I play the piano. I have friends who play horns, flutes, violins, and guitars. Sometimes we play together, but it is usually too hard to get everyone in one place. Second, an orchestra would be a great after-school activity for some students. Not everyone likes to do sports after school. Students should have the choice of playing music. Finally, music is an excellent way to bring people together. We could hold one or two concerts each year. The other students, parents, and family members would enjoy hearing us play. I hope you will let us organize an orchestra for our school.

    Yours truly,

Shannon Jordan

Focus/Ideas Focused on the request, supported with logical reasons

Organization/Paragraphs Clear introduction, transitions indicate reasons in order from least to most important

Voice Strong voice indicates reasonable, committed personality

Word Choice Uses persuasive words *(should, excellent)*

Sentences Varied, clear sentences with good rhythms

Conventions No errors

Persuasive Writing Model *Score 3*

Dear Mr. Gregory,

    Our school has a lot of good spellers. That is why a school spelling bee is a great idea. Students from each grade could compeat and pick two or three winners. Then the winners from all the grades could compeat in one big spelling bee or maybe grades 1 and 2, 3 and 4, and 5 and 6 could go together. The whole school and parents could come to the autorium and watch the spellers. This would be fun and educational and it would encourage kids to be good spellers.

    Yours truly,

    Matt Sanchez

Focus/Ideas Focused on the request, some distracting information on procedures

Organization/Paragraphs Good introduction and conclusion, reasons need better transitions and organization

Voice Believable, enthusiastic voice

Word Choice Good use of verbs *(compete, encourage)*; some use of persuasive words *(great idea)*

Sentences Several stringy sentences with unclear connecting words *(. . . or maybe grades 1 and 2, 3 and 4, . . .)*

Conventions Some missing commas in compound sentences; some spelling errors *(compeat, autorium)*

Persuasive Writing Model *Score 2*

Dear Ms. Lee,

   Can our school have a school Fair this year? I know we havnt had one for the last two years becuase it costs a lot. But it is really fun. The students will do the work it will not cost much. We will plan the games and set up the classrooms for them. We will get our parents to help us. They will make bake goods and help set up the games. Theyll also help run the games. Could we have the Fair on a saturday in February? Becuase that is a quiet month. Please let us do this becuase it is really fun.

                Yours truly,

                Rodney Jackson

Focus/Ideas Focused on the request

Organization/Paragraphs Needs clear arrangement of reasons from least important to most important

Voice Feelings about topic communicated

Word Choice Limited, dull word choice (*please, fun*); no persuasive words; repetition (*it is really fun*)

Sentences Little sentence variety

Conventions Run-on sentence and a fragment; lack of apostrophes for contractions (*havnt, theyll*); spelling and capitalization errors (*becuase, Fair, saturday*)

Persuasive Writing Model *Score 1*

Dear Mrs. Brady

   I thik we should be abel to have recess after lunch. Instad of just go back to class after lunch. We allredy have two recesses. But the problm is it is too hard to go rite back to work after eating. A little time to relax after eating. Evryone thiks this a good idea.

                                       Tara Schmidt

Focus/Ideas   Clear request, but not enough focused reasons

Organization/Paragraphs   Reasons not organized; no transitions

Voice Identifiable voice

Word Choice   Limited word choice; use of persuasive word *should*

Sentences   Little natural flow; fragments

Conventions   Many misspellings; does not observe letter format; awkward constructions *(Instad of just go back to class);* omitted words *(this a good idea)*

Expository Writing *Scoring Rubric*

Score	4	3	2	1
Focus/Ideas	Excellent explanation; main idea developed with strong details	Good explanation of main idea; details that mostly support it	Some focus on main idea, few supporting details	Main idea unfocused or lacking; few supporting details
Organization/ Paragraphs	Main idea in clear topic sentence; details in time order; appropriate connecting words	Adequate topic sentence; most details in correct order; some connecting words	Topic sentence, important details missing or in wrong order; few connecting words	No clear order to details or connecting words to show relationships; no clear topic sentence
Voice	Engaging, but serious and rather formal	Mostly serious, but with some inappropriate shifts	Voice not always appropriate to subject matter	Voice lacking or inappropriate
Word Choice	Carefully chosen, precise words	Topic portrayed with clear language	Some vague, repetitive, or incorrect words	Dull language; very limited word choices
Sentences	Well-crafted, varied sentences	Accurate sentence construction; some variety	Little variety; overly simple constructions, some errors	Many fragments, run-ons; sense hard to follow
Conventions	Excellent control of all mechanical aspects of writing	Few mechanical errors	Some distracting mechanical errors	Many errors in mechanics that prevent understanding

Following are four models that respond to a prompt. Each model has been given a score, based on the rubric.

Writing Prompt Think of a natural feature such as a mountain, body of water, or canyon. Write a paragraph explaining some important facts about it. For example, you might include information about how it was formed or what it is used for.

Expository Writing Model *Score 4*

The Grand Canyon is one of the great natural wonders of the world. Located in Arizona, it is 277 miles long and one mile deep in some places. The widest parts of the canyon are 18 miles wide. The Colorado River flows at the bottom of the canyon. How was the canyon formed? Erosion by the river created it millions of years ago. The rocks of the canyon walls are many shades of red, yellow, and brown. The canyon is so beautiful and so enormous that millions of people visit it every year. They can drive on roads around the canyon or hike on trails. Adventurous visitors can ride mules all the way down the canyon to the bottom. We are lucky to have such an amazing place in our country.

Focus/Ideas   Focused on the topic, supported with many facts and details

Organization/Paragraphs   Good introduction and conclusion; logical arrangement of details

Voice   Knowledgeable voice

Word Choice   Precise word choice and images *(many shades of red, yellow, and brown)*

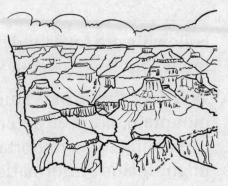

Sentences   Clear sentences of varied lengths and kinds

Conventions   Excellent control

Expository Writing Model *Score 3*

The Mississippi River is one of the chief Rivers in the United States. The name <u>Mississippi</u> comes from an Indian word that means "big river." The Mississippi starts in Minnesota and flows south all the way to the Gulf of Mexico. It goes 2,348 miles. Ships carry goods down the River. It's widest part is 4,500 feet at Cairo, Illinois. One interesting thing about the Mississippi River is that it forms the boundarys of many states such as Illinois, Kentucky, Missouri, and Arkansas. That's what I know about the Mississippi.

Focus/Ideas   Focused on the topic and supported with many details

Organization/Paragraphs   Needs transitions to make organization of details logical; weak conclusion

Voice   Trustworthy voice, needs more individuality

Word Choice   Precise verbs (*flows, forms*)

Sentences   Varied sentence lengths; many begin with *the*

Conventions   Mistakes with apostrophes (*It's widest part*) and capitalization (*Rivers, River*), spelling error (*boundarys*)

Expository Writing Model *Score 2*

> Mount Shasta is a moutain. It is in northern California. About 14,000 feet high. The resons it is famous is it has twin peeks. They are both volcanos. But they dont erupt. The second peek is 2,500 feet lower than the main one. The moutain is located in north central California. Mount Shasta is high and it is very beautiful.

Focus/Ideas   Focused on the topic but needs more supporting details

Organization/Paragraphs   Topic sentence included; details need more logical organization

Voice   No strong voice; reads like a list of facts

Word Choice   Limited word choice (*high, beautiful*), some wordiness

Sentences   Fragment (*About 14,000 feet high*); short, choppy sentences that could be combined

Conventions   Many misspellings, subject-verb agreement error (*reasons . . . is*)

Expository Writing Model *Score 1*

Lake Michigan is near us it is big it is a Great lake it is the thrid bigest. It is totaly in the United states it is not in canada at all. Did you know a ship cold go all the way from Lake michigan to the gulf of Mexico.

Focus/Ideas   Generally focused on the topic

Organization/Paragraphs   No logical organization, no introduction or conclusion

Voice   Writer not involved except in final sentence

Word Choice   Limited, dull word choice

Sentences   Run-ons

Conventions   Incorrect end punctuation; many misspellings; errors in capitalization; no paragraph indent

Evaluate Your Writing

You can evaluate your own writing by reading it over carefully. Think about what is good as well as what you can improve. As you read, ask yourself the following questions.

How does my writing sound?   Read it aloud to find out.

- If it sounds choppy, you might combine short sentences.
- Are there many sentences strung together with *and, because,* or *then?* "Unhook" a long stringy sentence by separating it into several sentences.
- Do most sentences begin with *I, the, it, she,* or *he?* Think of other ways to begin these sentences. Simply rearranging words might do the trick.
- Do ideas seem connected? If not, add transition words or phrases such as *finally* or *on the other hand*. These words connect ideas and help your sentences flow.

Is the style appropriate?   Who is your audience? (friends, your principal, a newspaper editor) What is your purpose? (to inform, to persuade, to entertain) Sentence fragments, informal language, and slang may be appropriate for e-mails or quick notes among friends. A more formal style suits written assignments.

Does your writing address the assignment?

- Look for key words in the writing prompt. For example:

    Compare and contrast a bike and a car.
    Tell two similarities and two differences.

    Topic: bike and car

    What you need to do: Compare and contrast

    What to include: Two similarities and two differences

- Other kinds of key words in writing prompts include *describe*, *explain*, *summarize*, *examples*, *why*, and *how*.

Is your writing focused? Are all the sentences about the main idea? Take out or refocus sentences that wander off into unimportant details.

Is there enough elaboration and support? Your writing may be unclear if you don't elaborate on your ideas. Supply information that readers need to know.

- Use sensory details to make your writing seem fresh and to give readers pictures, but avoid sounding flowery.
- If you give an opinion, supply strong supporting reasons.
- Expand on a main idea with several telling details.
- When necessary, define a term or give examples.

Is your beginning strong? Does a question, a surprising fact, or an amusing detail capture a reader's interest?

Is your ending satisfying? A conclusion may restate the main idea in a new way, tell what you feel or what you have learned, or pose a question to readers to think about. Whatever it does, it should signal that you have finished.

Have you used effective words—and not too many of them? Have you chosen your words carefully?

- Strong verbs, precise nouns, and vivid adjectives make your writing clear and lively.
- Are there awkward phrases you can replace with a word or two? For example, replace *due to the fact that* with *because* and *at this point in time* with *now*.

Check List

- [ ] My writing sounds smooth and easy to read.
- [ ] I have used an appropriate style for my audience and purpose.
- [ ] My writing addresses the prompt or assignment.
- [ ] My writing is focused.
- [ ] I have used enough elaboration and support.
- [ ] I have a strong beginning.
- [ ] I have a satisfying conclusion.
- [ ] I have used effective words and avoided wordiness.

Grammar and Writing Lessons

Sentences

A **sentence** tells a complete thought. It names someone or something and tells what that person or thing is or does. An incomplete sentence is called a **fragment**.

Sentence The girls ate strawberries.
Fragment A farmer in the big field.

Words in a sentence are in an order that makes sense. A sentence always begins with a capital letter and ends with an end mark.

A Write *S* if the group of words is a sentence. Write *F* if the group of words is a fragment.

1. The bakery sells fresh bread.
2. Serving lunch at the café.
3. The banker eats there each day.
4. At a quiet table in the corner.
5. Sometimes the miners come to town.
6. The shops are busy.
7. Selling tools and groceries.
8. Everyone works hard all week.
9. Each person has a job.
10. In town or on a farm.
11. The farmer rests.
12. Out in the field under a tree.

B Write the group of words in each pair that is a sentence.

1. Who will build a store?
Selling food and other goods?

2. Need cloth for shirts and pants.
One shop sells bolts of cloth.

3. Builders, cooks, and bankers.
A new town needs many workers.

4. Soon the town will be full of people.
Going to town on errands.

5. Milk, eggs, bread, and a toothbrush.
People rush from store to store.

6. Did I forget something?
Ten things on my shopping list.

C Add your own words to make complete sentences. Write the new sentences. Remember to use capital letters and punctuation marks.

7. Apple pie ____.

8. The kitchen in my house ____.

9. ____ tastes good after lunch.

10. ____ are easy to bake.

11. All kinds of fruit ____.

12. ____ is my favorite thing to cook.

13. I like ____.

14. For lunch, we ____.

Test Preparation

 Write the letter of the sentence that has correct capitalization and punctuation.

1. A What is a ghost town.
   B what is a ghost town?
   C what is a ghost town.
   D What is a ghost town?

2. A Miners didn't find gold
   B Miners didn't find gold.
   C miners didn't find gold.
   D miners didn't find gold

3. A They had to move away
   B they had to move away
   C they had to move away.
   D They had to move away.

4. A They left their houses
   B they left their houses.
   C They left their houses.
   D they left their houses

 Write the letter of the complete sentence.

5. A Houses and stores.
   B Standing in many towns.
   C Buildings stayed empty.
   D Weren't needed anymore.

6. A People went to cities.
   B Working in other jobs.
   C Gave up dreams.
   D Getting rich quickly.

7. A Towns with houses and shops.
   B Some towns didn't last long.
   C Families of the miners.
   D People suddenly gone.

8. A In many areas of the West.
   B Empty towns still stand.
   C Streets and buildings.
   D Looking broken down.

Review

Write *S* if the group of words is a sentence. Write *F* if the group of words is a fragment.

1. Drake explored California.

2. Sailed on the coast in 1579.

3. Many people from Spain.

4. They settled in villages.

5. Big ranches with cattle.

6. American trappers in the 1800s.

7. They came to California too.

8. Many pioneers soon settled there.

9. Farming and ranching.

10. Became a state in 1850.

Decide whether each group of words is a sentence or a fragment. If it is a sentence, write the sentence with correct capitalization and punctuation. If it is a fragment, write *F*.

11. a man owned land in California in 1848

12. wanted to build a sawmill

13. a worker found gold in Sutter's river

14. told everyone about the discovery

15. thousands of people rushed to Sutter's mill

16. a few people made their fortunes

17. returned home with no gold

18. others opened businesses

Voice

> **Voice** shows a writer's personality. It shows feelings and makes one person's writing sound different from everyone else's.

Write a word from the box to describe the voice of each writer.

persuasive	serious	imaginative

1. Are you tired of working hard every day? Would you like to make a lot of money? Then come to the gold mines of California. After you pan for gold for a few days, you may never have to work again. The gold you find will buy you a beautiful new home and time to enjoy it.

2. Can you picture a gold miner in California in 1848? "Yahoo! I just found gold at Sutter's mill. It was a nugget as big as a loaf of bread! I will take it to town. By this time tomorrow I will be rich! I will probably never have to work again!"

3. The Gold Rush brought many people to California. They all hoped to find gold and get rich. But many of them did not find gold. Still, they decided to stay in California. The land was rich even if the gold mines were not. They stayed and built homes, farms, and towns.

Would you have gone to California to find gold? Write two or three sentences telling why or why not. Use a voice that helps express your feelings about mining for gold.

Character Description

> A **character description** makes a person or story character come alive for the reader. It vividly describes the person's actions and character traits.

Topic sentence "sets up" three character traits.

Detail sentences tell actions for each trait.

Conclusion tells writer's feelings about the character.

My Favorite Artist

My Aunt Jen is the most creative, patient, and fun person I know. She is an artist. She usually paints pictures of places. Aunt Jen makes a place seem real and inviting. I always wish I could somehow get inside the painting and experience that place.

Aunt Jen is a busy artist, but she finds time to teach others. She gives me an art lesson each Saturday. She is patient even when I am all thumbs with my paintbrush.

Finally, Aunt Jen is fun. She loves art, but she also likes to sing and play catch in the backyard. Aunt Jen is one of my favorite people to spend time with. I want to be like her when I grow up.

Subjects and Predicates

A sentence has a **subject** and a **predicate.** The subject is the sentence part that tells whom or what the sentence is about. All the words in the subject are called the **complete subject.** The predicate is the sentence part that tells what the subject is or does. All the words in the predicate are called the **complete predicate.**

In the following sentences, the complete subject is underlined once. The complete predicate is underlined twice.

Most people learn something each day.
The boy on that bike is my brother.

A Write the complete subject of each sentence.

1. We find knowledge in many places.

2. The students in our class ask questions.

3. The library has books about many subjects.

4. Teachers help students with their lessons.

5. Books about animals are my favorites.

6. My two friends like mysteries.

Write the complete predicate of each sentence.

7. The class studied whales.

8. The school librarian knows all about caves.

9. James read about pirates.

10. People learn about animals at the zoo.

B Write each sentence. Underline the complete subject. Circle the complete predicate.

1. The farmers raise goats.
2. They sell the goats' wool.
3. Wool from goats feels soft and fluffy.
4. Mom made a wool sweater.
5. Some people drink goat's milk.
6. Goats and sheep are important farm animals.
7. Sheep have thick, curly fur.
8. My new winter coat is made from sheep's wool.

C Add a predicate to each subject to make a complete sentence. Write the sentence with correct punctuation.

9. My favorite farm animal ____.
10. Farms in my state ____.
11. Wool ____.
12. Cows ____.

Add a subject to each predicate to make a complete sentence. Write the sentence with correct punctuation.

13. ____ wears sweaters.
14. ____ keeps me warm.
15. ____ is cold in winter.
16. ____ feels good in winter.

Test Preparation

✓ Write the letter of the complete subject of each sentence.

1. All of my friends like gifts.

   A All
   B my friends
   C All of my friends
   D friends like gifts

2. Birthday presents are nice surprises.

   A Birthday
   B Birthday presents
   C presents are
   D nice surprises

3. We get gifts every day.

   A We
   B We get
   C get
   D get gifts

4. Some gifts are not wrapped up.

   A Some gifts
   B gifts
   C gifts are
   D not wrapped up

✓ Write the letter of the complete predicate of each sentence.

5. My favorite gift was a bicycle.

   A My favorite
   B favorite gift
   C gift was
   D was a bicycle

6. The bicycle goes fast.

   A The bicycle
   B bicycle goes
   C goes fast
   D goes

Review

Write the complete subject of each sentence.

1. Carpets make floors soft and colorful.
2. Animal skin rugs covered cave floors.
3. People in the Middle East wove rugs long ago.
4. Rugs from different countries have different patterns.
5. That Persian rug has birds and leaves.
6. The rug in my room is blue with white dots.

Write the complete predicate of each sentence.

7. Bright colors make that rug unusual.
8. The Chinese rug is red and blue.
9. American colonists made braided rugs.
10. Machines make many rugs today.
11. People weave rugs by hand also.
12. Those rugs last for many years.

Write each sentence. Underline the complete subject. Circle the complete predicate.

13. Weavers made this rug from wool.
14. The rug looks soft and colorful.
15. The pattern has squares and circles.
16. People in France wove the rug.
17. Our family room needs a rug like this.
18. The old rug is thin and worn.

Repetition and Rhyme

> In **repetition,** a writer repeats words or groups of words. In **rhyme,** the ending sounds of two words are alike. Repetition and rhyme make songs and poems fun to read or sing.

 Write the repeated words or groups of words in each story.

1. The goat grew the wool. A farmer cut the wool. That spinner spun the wool. The woman knit the wool. And on a cold winter day, I wore the wool!

2. The kids were messy. The kids were playful. The kids were covered with soft fur. The kids were baby goats!

Write the words that rhyme in each poem.

3. My sweater's made of bright red wool.
It will unravel if you pull!

4. The sheep and goats are free to roam,
But when the sun sets, they come home.

5. The farmer went up to the goat
And said, "It's time to trim your coat."
The goat went on his happy way
And thought, "He won't catch me today!"

Write two lines about animals on a farm. Make the lines rhyme. Repeat at least one word or group of words.

Song

> A **song** can describe a feeling or event that is important to the writer. It uses repetition and rhyme to vividly express the writer's personality.

Repetition such as *funny dog* makes the song fun.

Rhymes (*dog/log, pup/up, ball/fall, pet/yet*) make the song lively.

Repetition such as *crazy pet* shows the writer's personality.

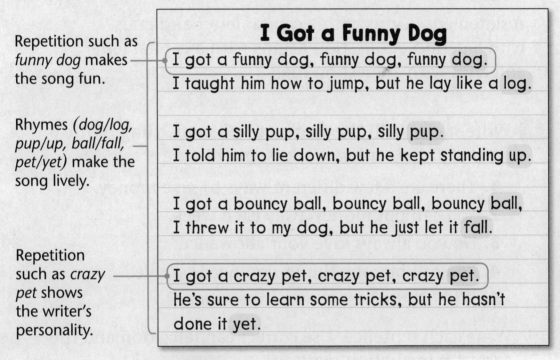

I Got a Funny Dog

I got a funny dog, funny dog, funny dog.
I taught him how to jump, but he lay like a log.

I got a silly pup, silly pup, silly pup.
I told him to lie down, but he kept standing up.

I got a bouncy ball, bouncy ball, bouncy ball,
I threw it to my dog, but he just let it fall.

I got a crazy pet, crazy pet, crazy pet.
He's sure to learn some tricks, but he hasn't done it yet.

Statements and Questions

A sentence that tells something is a **statement**. A sentence that asks something is a **question.**

Statement Most people save money.

Question Do you save money?

A statement begins with a capital letter and ends with a period. A question begins with a capital letter and ends with a question mark.

A Write *statement* if the sentence tells something. Write *question* if the sentence asks something.

1. There are a few different ways to save money.

2. You can put money away each week.

3. Do you always save your allowance?

4. You can buy the things you need on sale.

5. What is the best way to save money?

Write each sentence. Use correct capitalization and the correct punctuation mark.

6. my sister Annie saves one dollar each week

7. frank does not spend money on candy

8. did you save your birthday money

9. could we put the money in the bank

10. saving money can be fun

B Use one word from the box to make each statement into a question. Write the new sentences. Use correct capitalization and punctuation. You can use a word more than once.

can	will	should	do

Example: You need money in the future.
Answer: Will you need money in the future?

1. You put money in the bank.

2. The dollars add up over the years.

3. You save money for college.

4. Your friends save money in the bank too.

5. The banks help you save money.

6. You save as much as you can.

C Add words to expand each item below into an interesting sentence. Each item will tell you whether to write a statement or a question.

7. Statement: tellers work

8. Question: banks pay

9. Statement: banks lend

10. Statement: families save

11. Question: boys and girls learn

12. Question: money help

Test Preparation

 Write the letter of the sentence that is written correctly.

1. **A** the colonists didn't make coins.
   B The colonists didn't make coins
   C The colonists didn't make coins.
   D the colonists didn't make coins

2. **A** How did they buy things.
   B How did they buy things?
   C how did they buy things?
   D How did they buy things

3. **A** They traded goods
   B they traded goods?
   C they traded goods.
   D They traded goods.

4. **A** What did they trade
   B What did they trade.
   C what did they trade?
   D What did they trade?

5. **A** Did they trade crops.
   B Did they trade crops?
   C did they trade crops.
   D did they trade crops?

6. **A** They also traded furs.
   B they also traded furs.
   C they also traded furs
   D They also traded furs

7. **A** Some people had Spanish money
   B some people had Spanish money.
   C Some people had Spanish money.
   D some people had Spanish money

8. **A** Was it made of gold.
   B was it made of gold
   C was it made of gold?
   D Was it made of gold?

Review

✓ Write *statement* if the sentence tells something. Write *question* if the sentence asks something.

1. Who made the first money?

2. The Chinese used paper money long ago.

3. Did American colonists use paper money?

4. They had no bills until the 1700s.

5. They traded goods instead of money.

✓ Write each sentence with the correct punctuation mark.

6. Did the first Americans have banks

7. Most colonists lived on farms

8. Alexander Hamilton wanted large banks

9. What did Thomas Jefferson think about banks

10. Jefferson thought farmers didn't need banks

✓ Use a word from the box to make each statement into a question. Write the new sentence. Use correct capitalization and punctuation. You can use a word more than once.

can	will	should	do

11. You know what kinds of money other countries have.

12. You remember that Mexico uses *pesos*.

13. You spend dollars in Mexico.

14. You change your dollars to *pesos*.

15. You buy things in Mexico.

Time-order Words

> **Time-order words,** such as *then* and *today,* tell you when something happens.
>
> <u>After</u> I got my allowance, I went to the store.

Write the time-order word in each sentence.

1. Yesterday Jon had a money-making idea.
2. First he bought some sturdy paper.
3. Then he bought some wooden sticks.
4. Next he picked up a ball of string.
5. He looked for some colorful rags later.
6. Jon worked in the garage afterwards.
7. Finally, he had made six kites.
8. Tomorrow he will sell the kites to his friends.

Add a time-order word to each sentence. Write the sentences.

9. ___ Jon sold the six kites.
10. ___ he made some more kites.
11. ___ he sold all those kites too.
12. ___ he will make something else.

Write two or three sentences about a time when you sold or bought something. Use two or more time-order words to tell when something happened.

Math Story

> A **story** tells about some related events that happened to someone. A math story tells about something that happened that had to do with numbers and math.

Last fall tells when the story takes place.

First and *next* show the sequence of events.

Questions give the paragraph variety.

A Wrapping-Paper Problem

Last fall my soccer team needed money for uniforms. Each player would sell ten rolls of wrapping paper for $4 each. First, I sold three rolls to the Hongs next door. Next, the Lanes bought two rolls. Mrs. Sanchez also bought two rolls. On the way home I saw Mr. Collins. He bought three rolls. How many rolls of wrapping paper had I sold? How much money did I earn for uniforms?

Commands and Exclamations

A sentence that tells someone to do something is a **command.** A sentence that shows strong feelings is an **exclamation.**

Command	Put a dollar on the counter. Please give me a quarter.
Exclamation	What a bright penny that is! I can't wait to show it to you!

Some commands begin with *please*. Commands usually end with periods. The subject of a command is *you*. The word *you* is not written or said, but it is understood. Exclamations can express feelings such as surprise, anger, or excitement. Exclamations begin with a capital letter and end with an exclamation mark.

A Write *command* if the sentence is a command or *exclamation* if the sentence is an exclamation.

1. Please give me change for a dollar.
2. Put the money in your pocket.
3. What a big bag of pennies that is!
4. Count the pennies carefully.
5. I am so tired of counting!
6. That castle is so beautiful!
7. Please take a picture of the gardens.
8. How expensive it must be!

B Write the sentences. Add the correct end punctuation. Write *C* if the sentence is a command and *E* if the sentence is an exclamation.

1. What a great coin collection you have
2. I can't believe that penny is 100 years old
3. Look at this old nickel
4. Start a coin collection of your own
5. Look for interesting coins everywhere
6. You will have a wonderful time
7. Begin the search today

C Write a sentence for each item. Follow the directions.

8. Write an exclamation about an interesting collection.
9. Write a command about how to collect something.
10. Write a command to someone in a store.
11. Write an exclamation about finding something special at a garage sale.
12. Write a command to someone who wants to see your collection.
13. Write an exclamation about your favorite toy.
14. Write a command about how to care for a collection.

Test Preparation

 Write the letter of the answer that best completes the kind of sentence in ( ).

1. Tell me about your ___ (command)

    A job.   **C** job?

    B job   **D** Job!

2. ___ an interesting job you have! (exclamation)

    A what!   **C** What!

    B what   **D** What

3. Explain how you became an animal ___ (command)

    A trainer   **C** trainer?

    B trainer.   **D** trainer!

4. What beautiful animals you ___ (exclamation)

    A have!   **C** have

    B have.   **D** have?

5. Let me pet an ___ (command)

    A elephant! **C** elephant

    B elephant. **D** elephant?

6. That elephant is ___ (exclamation)

    A huge   **C** huge!

    B huge?   **D** huge.

7. ___ help me reach the elephant's ear. (command)

    A Please.   **C** Please

    B please   **D** Please!

8. ___ rough the elephant's skin is! (exclamation)

    A How!   **C** How

    B how!   **D** how

9. Show me the elephant's ___ (command)

    A food!   **C** food

    B food.   **D** food?

10. What fun this has ___ (exclamation)

    A been!   **C** been.

    B been?   **D** been

Review

✓ Write *command* if the sentence is a command or *exclamation* if the sentence is an exclamation.

1. Show me your silver dollars.
2. How shiny they are!
3. That coin is very strange!
4. Turn the coin over.
5. What an unusual picture that is!
6. Please put the coin back.

✓ Write the sentences. Add the correct end punctuation. Write *C* if the sentence is a command and *E* if the sentence is an exclamation.

7. Learn about coins at the library
8. I can't believe there are so many books about coins
9. Look in the index for facts about dimes
10. That's the strangest dime I've ever seen
11. Don't clean your coins
12. Don't handle them too much
13. Collecting coins is a great hobby
14. Arrange the coins in the school display case
15. What an artistic arrangement you made
16. You have the best collection in the whole school
17. Please let me hold that coin
18. That coin is very heavy

Commands and Exclamations

Sometimes you will use **commands** and **exclamations** in writing. If you want to tell someone to do something, you can use a command. If you want to express a strong feeling such as surprise, anger, or excitement, you can use an exclamation. Commands and exclamations add variety to your writing.

 Write the name of a kind of writing in which each command might appear. Choose a name from the box.

> story   persuasive letter   ad

1. Think how much you would enjoy riding a Model K bike.

2. Please consider me for the job because I am a very hard worker.

3. Read this strange tale of a talking fish.

Write the name of a feeling that each exclamation shows.

4. I found a rare silver dollar at the coin fair!

5. Someone bought it before I had a chance!

6. My dad promised to take me to next month's fair!

Imagine you have found a wonderful addition for your collection. Write a command and an exclamation about the item.

E-mail

An **e-mail** is a note or letter sent to someone on a computer. Often brief and informal, e-mails are an easy way to keep in touch.

An e-mail to a friend uses informal words. A business e-mail is more formal.

These are commands.

Exclamations express the writer's excitement.

Subject: New Pet
Date: Thursday, May 16, 2007 6:22:17 PM
From: Jane.Sherman@netbiz.com
To: Christina.Sanchez@abc.net

Hey! Guess what happened. I saw a cute kitten on my way home from school. It had soft fur with gray and white stripes. It was sitting all by itself on the sidewalk near my house. I took it home. It followed me all over the house, meowing in a tiny voice. My mom said we should look for its owner. We took the kitten down the street. Soon we saw our neighbor. She was so happy to see the kitten! Guess what she said. She said I could buy the kitten for $10. I had just earned $10 for cleaning the garage. This was such a lucky day for me! If you come over tomorrow, you can see Zippy.

Compound Sentences

A **simple sentence** has one subject and one predicate. **A compound** sentence contains two simple sentences joined by a comma and a word such as *and, but,* or *or.*

Simple Sentence The boy helped his mother.

Simple Sentence His mother got him a bicycle.

Compound Sentence The boy helped his mother, and his mother got him a bicycle.

The two parts of a compound sentence have ideas that make sense together. A comma goes after the first sentence, before the word *and, but,* or *or.*

A Write *S* if the sentence is a simple sentence. Write *C* if the sentence is a compound sentence.

1. The family had a farm.

2. The boy planted beans, and his mom planted pumpkins.

3. The family ate bananas and spinach.

4. The spinach tasted good, but the bananas tasted better.

5. The boy picked the crops, and his father sold them.

6. A wheelbarrow carries crops.

7. You can pick peas, or you can dig sweet potatoes.

8. It rains in spring, and the crops grow quickly.

9. Coffee grows on trees, and pumpkins grow on vines.

10. Work on a farm is often hard.

B Write each compound sentence. Add a comma to punctuate the sentence correctly.

1. Rob walks to school and Will rides his bike.

2. Bicycle accidents are common but Will rides carefully.

3. Will signals his turns and he always walks his bike across the street.

4. Will rides his bike on weekends or he may hike with his family.

5. Will's brother doesn't like bike trips but Will enjoys them.

6. Rob will buy a bike or he may get one for his birthday next month.

C Use the word in ( ) to combine each pair of simple sentences. Write the compound sentence.

7. The first bicycle was wooden. It looked like a scooter. (and)

8. Another bike had handlebars. It had no pedals. (but)

9. The high-wheeler had a big front wheel. The back wheel was small. (but)

10. People rode bikes for fun. Soon the roads were full of them. (and)

11. People might walk to work. They might bike. (or)

12. You can see early bikes at a museum. You might find them in an antique shop. (or)

Test Preparation

 Write the letter of the words that complete each sentence correctly.

1. Bike races are ___ are also challenging.

   A popular, And they

   B popular, and they

   C popular and they

   D popular or they

2. Some races are ___ are very long.

   A short and some

   B short, And some

   C short, but some

   D short or some

3. Some races include ___ do not.

   A teams, but others

   B teams or others

   C teams and others

   D teams, But others

4. Some races are ___ are run on special tracks.

   A indoors and they

   B indoors but they

   C indoors, and they

   D indoors, And they

5. Others are ___ go many miles.

   A outdoors. and they

   B outdoors but they

   C outdoors and they

   D outdoors, and they

6. Racers may train ___ use indoor tracks.

   A outdoors and they may

   B outdoors or they may

   C outdoors but they may

   D outdoors, or they may

Review

✓ Write *S* if the sentence is a simple sentence. Write *C* if the sentence is a compound sentence.

   1. We had a bicycle race through our town.

   2. I did not ride in the race, but Carla did.

   3. The race began on Main Street, and it went for five miles.

   4. Carla got a good start.

   5. Carla's friends stood on the street, and they cheered her on.

   6. There were many racers, and they were all fast.

   7. Carla looked strong, but she was stuck in fourth place.

   8. The race was nearly over, and Carla finally pulled ahead.

   9. Carla crossed the finish line first.

   10. We all had lemonade and ice cream after the race.

✓ Choose one of the words in ( ) to combine each pair of simple sentences. Write the compound sentence.

   11. Julio wants a new racing bike. It is costly. (but, or)

   12. He has a job. It is hard to save money. (but, and)

   13. He goes to the shop often. He looks at all the bikes. (or, and)

   14. He will get a red bike. He will choose a blue one. (or, but)

   15. He will soon have enough money. He will finally get his bike. (and, but)

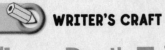

Show, Don't Tell

> When you write about yourself,
> *show*—don't *tell*—how you feel.
>
> **No** I was nervous.
> **Yes** My voice croaked, and my knees trembled.

 Use words from the box or your own words to improve sentences 1–4.

packed with tents and food	chattered and cheered
shimmered like glass	jumped out of bed

(1) I (woke up excited) ____. It was the first day at Camp Kanaho. **(2)** The lake (looked pretty) ____. **(3)** The kids (were noisy) ____. **(4)** Canoes were (ready) ____.

Read the pair of sentences. Write the letter of the sentence that *shows* instead of *tells*.

5. A Marisa was excited and happy about the surprise party.

  B Marisa squealed and jumped up and down when her friends threw a surprise party for her.

6. A Fog was in the valley and made it difficult to see.

  B Fog covered the valley like a thick white blanket.

Imagine that you are in a strange place, such as a jungle, attic, or cave. Describe what you see, feel, hear, touch, and smell.

Writing for Tests

Prompt Think about the <u>first time</u> you did something. It might have been going to a new school, moving to a new place, or joining a team. Write a <u>narrative paragraph</u> to a <u>friend</u> showing how you felt.

The First Game

Details create a vivid mood. Specific verbs paint word pictures.

   The air chilled my nose and hands on Saturday morning. The wet grass squeaked under my new shoes. But I didn't even notice the weather. It was my first soccer game!

Writer *shows* that she was early and nervous.

I paced around the empty field as I waited for the rest of the team to arrive. Soon the game had started. I lost all track of time as I joined the herd of players racing up and down the field. Suddenly I got the chance I was waiting for. The ball was at my feet, and the goal was straight ahead. I took a deep breath and aimed for the goal. The goalkeeper dove for the ball, but she was too late. I scored a goal!

Writer *shows* that she felt proud and excited.

The crowd on the sidelines roared, but I didn't even notice it. The roar in my ears came from my own heart.

Common and Proper Nouns

A **common noun** names any person, place, or thing. A **proper noun** names a particular person, place, or thing. Proper nouns begin with capital letters.

Common Nouns   These <u>birds</u> live in cold <u>places</u>.

Proper Nouns   It is cold in <u>Antarctica</u> in <u>July</u>.

The names of days, months, and holidays are proper nouns. They begin with capital letters. Capitalize each important word in a proper noun: *Fourth of July.*

A Write *C* if the underlined noun is a common noun. Write *P* if the underlined noun is a proper noun.

1. Penguins have black and white <u>feathers</u>.
2. Some penguins live in zoos in the <u>United States</u>.
3. Penguins have webbed <u>feet</u>.
4. <u>New Zealand</u> has many penguins.
5. This penguin hatched in <u>August</u>.
6. Penguins eat fish from the <u>water</u>.
7. There is much food in the <u>ocean</u>.
8. Some penguins live in <u>Australia</u>.
9. <u>Seals</u> and whales live in Antarctica.
10. Did you see penguins at the zoo on <u>Labor Day</u>?

B Write the headings *Common Nouns* and *Proper Nouns* on your paper. Write each noun in the sentences under the correct heading. There are nine common nouns and three proper nouns.

1. Many birds can be found in Antarctica.

2. Most birds do not live near the South Pole in winter.

3. Their home then is far across the ocean.

4. South America is one destination.

5. The sea can also be a source of food.

C Write the sentences. Capitalize the proper nouns correctly. The number in ( ) tells how many proper nouns are in each sentence.

6. We left on our trip to alaska on new year's day. (2)

7. Some whales and seals live in the pacific ocean. (1)

8. One day david and I took pictures of a whale. (1)

9. We saw a polar bear in january. (1)

10. It was near the coast of the arctic ocean. (1)

11. We saw many birds near the city of anchorage. (1)

12. They live in the pine forests in denali national park. (1)

13. Brown bears live on kodiak island. (1)

14. The largest glacier in north america is in alaska. (2)

15. Mr. murphy and I saw many glaciers. (1)

16. We stopped at sitka and ketchikan on our way home. (2)

Test Preparation

 Write the letter of the sentence that is written correctly.

1. **A** We saw cranes from florida.

B We saw Cranes from florida.

C We saw cranes from Florida.

D We saw Cranes from Florida.

2. **A** There is a zoo in san diego, california.

B There is a zoo in San Diego, California.

C There is a zoo in san Diego, california.

D There is a zoo in San Diego, california.

3. **A** We saw doves there on tuesday.

B We saw Doves there on Tuesday.

C We saw Doves there on tuesday.

D We saw doves there on Tuesday.

4. **A** Mr. lane showed us pete, a huge parrot.

B Mr. lane showed us Pete, a huge parrot.

C Mr. Lane showed us Pete, a huge parrot.

D Mr. Lane showed us Pete, a huge Parrot.

5. **A** Has Joey ever seen a Flamingo?

B Has joey ever seen a flamingo?

C Has joey ever seen a Flamingo?

D Has Joey ever seen a flamingo?

Review

Write *C* if the underlined noun is a common noun. Write *P* if the underlined noun is a proper noun.

1. Each region of the <u>United States</u> has unique birds.
2. Robins and sparrows live in cities like <u>Boston</u>.
3. <u>Wrens</u> and jays live in forests in the Northeast.
4. Owls live on the prairies of <u>Nebraska</u>.
5. Eagles live in the <u>deserts</u> of the Southwest.
6. Great blue herons fish in the lakes in <u>Texas</u>.
7. <u>Pelicans</u> fly over the Gulf of Mexico.
8. Many <u>birds</u> follow the Mississippi River.

Write the sentences. Capitalize the proper nouns correctly. The number in ( ) tells how many proper nouns are in each sentence.

9. Gray catbirds live in michigan. (1)
10. The painted bunting migrates to mexico each winter. (1)
11. Last year jamal and paul saw birds in louisiana. (3)
12. The ducks had flown from canada in late september. (2)
13. Mr. burns took pictures of roadrunners in arizona. (2)
14. The coast of the pacific ocean is home to many gulls. (1)
15. The rain forests of south america have amazing birds. (1)
16. The toucan lives in brazil. (1)
17. Last valentine's day adam saw a scarlet ibis. (2)
18. The bright red bird was in a swamp near the caribbean sea. (1)

Including Necessary Information

In a summary, a few sentences tell the main ideas of a story or article. To summarize, **include all necessary information** that readers need to understand what the article is about. Do not include unnecessary supporting details.

Write one or two sentences summarizing the necessary information in each paragraph.

1. Millions of years ago, penguins could fly. You can see the long black "wings" on the sides of their bodies. But their wings turned to flippers. Now penguins are excellent swimmers. Their flippers are strong paddles. Penguins' webbed feet also help them swim.

2. Few animals live in the center of Antarctica. But many live in the Antarctic Ocean and along the coast. Many whales go to Antarctica for the summer. The Antarctic fur seal lives on islands near Antarctica. Seals eat fish and squid from the ocean. Many birds, such as gulls and terns, also spend their summers in Antarctica. They nest on land. They get food from the ocean.

3. Antarctica is an unusual continent. About 98% of the continent is covered with an icecap. This is a thick layer of ice and snow. Big sheets of the icecap float in the water off the coast. These are called ice shelves. In summer, parts of the ice shelves break off. They form big, flat icebergs.

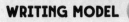

Summary

A **summary** tells the important ideas and information in an article, or it tells what happens in a story.

Writer describes only the most important events in the story's plot.

Strong verbs *visits*, *fears*, and *creates* make the summary clear and vivid.

The time-order words *after* and *soon* help make the order of events clear.

Summary—Charlotte's Web

Fern Arable wants to save Wilbur, a pig on her family's farm. He becomes her pet. Fern visits Wilbur often, even when he must live at her uncle's farm. Wilbur meets the farm animals, including Charlotte, a spider.

Wilbur fears he may soon be killed by the farmer. Charlotte creates something amazing to save him. The people find "Some Pig" and other messages written on Charlotte's web. Wilbur becomes famous. The animals decide that if Wilbur wins first prize at the County Fair, he will be saved forever. Wilbur wins a special prize thanks to Charlotte's messages. He is saved!

Charlotte is old. After laying many eggs, she dies. The spiders soon hatch. Charlotte's three daughters become Wilbur's friends. Charlotte's grandchildren and great-grandchildren take Charlotte's place as time passes. Yet Wilbur never forgets Charlotte.

Singular and Plural Nouns

A **singular noun** names only one person, place, or thing. A **plural noun** names more than one person, place, or thing.

Singular Nouns A tall <u>weed</u> sprouted beside the <u>creek</u>.

Plural Nouns <u>Grasses</u> grew among the <u>trees</u>.

Most nouns add -*s* to form the plural. Add -*es* to a noun that ends in *ch, sh, s, ss,* or *x: benches, wishes, gases, glasses, foxes.* When a noun ends in a consonant and *y*, change the *y* to *i* and then add -*es: cities.*

A Write *S* if the underlined noun is singular. Write *P* if the underlined noun is plural.

1. There are many <u>jobs</u> on the farm.
2. That job will take you one <u>day</u>.
3. Daniel picks <u>strawberries</u> with his brother.
4. The <u>apples</u> are not ripe yet.
5. Anita plants <u>bushes</u> each fall.
6. The <u>farmer</u> planted vegetables.
7. Tomatoes grow on long <u>vines</u>.
8. Onions and <u>carrots</u> grow under the ground.
9. Some beans grow on a tall <u>stalk</u>.
10. A <u>worker</u> is picking crops.

B Write the plural form of the noun in ( ).

1. James worked for Mr. Dixon for five (day) every week.
2. He planted (flower) in Mr. Dixon's garden.
3. He pulled weeds from the roses and (lily).
4. One day James trimmed tree (branch).
5. He cleaned the front and back (porch).
6. He took (stone) out of the soil.
7. He put them in big (box).
8. James discovered lovely ferns and (moss).
9. Mr. Dixon gave James some (daisy).
10. His mother arranged them in (bunch).
11. He gave them to the (lady) at his church.
12. They put the flowers in tall (vase).

C Complete each sentence by adding plural nouns. Write the new sentence.

13. The gardener planted ___ and ___ in the soil.
14. Insects such as ___ and ___ crawled in the garden.
15. Ms. Beasley grows vegetables, including ___ and ___, in her garden.
16. She needs tools, such as ___ and ___, to work in the garden.
17. She will make ___ and ___ with the fruits from her garden.
18. Ms. Beasley gives vegetables from her garden to everyone, including ___ and ___.

Test Preparation

✓ Write the letter of the plural form of each underlined noun.

1. Bob works on <u>ranch</u>.

   A ranchs   **C** ranches

   B ranch   **D** ranchies

2. He helps his <u>boss</u> each day.

   A bosss   **C** boss's

   B boss   **D** bosses

3. Bob trains <u>horse</u>.

   A horse   **C** horses

   B horse's   **D** horsies

4. He cares for cows and their <u>baby</u>.

   A babies   **C** babyss

   B babys   **D** babees

5. Sometimes <u>fox</u> come to the ranch.

   A foxs   **C** foxis

   B fox's   **D** foxes

6. Bob builds <u>fence</u> to keep them out.

   A fencs   **C** fencies

   B fences   **D** fencess

7. Bob trims the <u>bush</u>.

   A bushs   **C** bushes

   B bushess   **D** bush's

8. He is careful not to get <u>scratch</u>.

   A scratchs   **C** scratch's

   B scratchess   **D** scratches

Review

✔ Write the plural nouns in each sentence. The number in ( ) tells how many plural nouns are in each sentence.

1. Plump grapes grow on the vines. (2)
2. Workers walk beside the plants. (2)
3. They pull grapes from the branches with their fingers. (3)
4. They put pieces of fruit in boxes. (2)
5. They load the crates into trucks. (2)
6. Grocers put displays of fruit in their stores. (3)
7. Customers buy strawberries and cherries. (3)
8. Shoppers also buy blueberries and peaches. (3)
9. Clerks put the bags into the carts. (3)
10. Helpers take the groceries to the cars. (3)

✔ Write the plural form of the noun in ( ).

11. Mark works in the pineapple (field) in Hawaii.
12. He picks (pineapple) every day.
13. Helpers put the fruit into (basket).
14. They go to the fields in (bus).
15. The fruit is taken to the factory in (carton).
16. Workers cut the fruit into (slice).
17. The fruit is put into (can).
18. People put pineapple in fruit (salad).
19. They drink pineapple juice from (glass).
20. Chefs use pineapple in many (dish).

Eliminating Wordiness

Wordiness means using more words than needed.

Wordy I think the most important thing to remember when you clean your room is to dust each piece of furniture such as the desk, dresser, and night table.

Revised When you clean your room, dust all the furniture.

Follow these steps to eliminate wordiness:

- Use strong one-word verbs instead of phrases, for example, *remove* instead of *take off*.

- State each idea only once in as few words as possible.

- Delete wordy phrases such as *kind of* and *I think that*.

Rewrite each sentence to eliminate wordiness.

1. It seems to me that the job of babysitting is one of the hardest jobs in the whole wide world.

2. Little tiny kids run around like crazy some of the time and it seems like you have to keep your eye on them.

Write a tip about doing a job. Write it in a sentence that is not wordy.

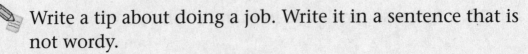

Rules

> **Rules** tell what people should do and shouldn't do. Rules are often written in a numbered list.

The rules are written as commands. The first word or phrase in each rule is a verb that tells readers what to do.

Rules include clear details. For example, #4 includes plural nouns that name specific things in a room.

Each rule is stated as briefly as possible.

Rules for Cleaning Your Room

1. Pick up toys, clothes, and books from your floor. Put each item in a drawer, in the closet, or on shelves.
2. Make your bed. Pull up the sheet, blanket, and bedspread smoothly. Fluff up the pillow.
3. Remove trash from your desk, floor, and other areas.
4. Straighten up the books, papers, and pencils on your desk.
5. Dust the desk, dresser, and night table.
6. Vacuum the floor.
7. Keep your room neat after you clean it.
8. Don't complain!

Irregular Plural Nouns

A plural noun names more than one person, place, or thing. Most nouns add -*s* to form the plural. An **irregular plural noun** has a special form for the plural.

Singular Nouns   An <u>ox</u> and a <u>sheep</u> live on the farm.

Irregular Plural Nouns   Three <u>oxen</u> and some <u>sheep</u> live on the farm.

Some nouns and their irregular plural forms are *child/ children, deer/deer, foot/feet, goose/geese, leaf/leaves, life/lives, man/men, mouse/mice, ox/oxen, sheep/sheep, tooth/teeth,* and *woman/women.*

A Write *S* if the underlined noun is singular. Write *P* if the underlined noun is plural.

1. Some <u>children</u> collect pets.

2. Carrie has four <u>mice</u>.

3. She has a pet <u>goose</u> in her yard.

4. Carrie wants some woolly <u>sheep</u>.

5. She even wants a <u>deer</u>.

6. We told the <u>woman</u> about our problem.

7. We could not rake all the <u>leaves</u>.

8. We can't run with leaves under our <u>feet</u>.

9. Some <u>men</u> brought machines to school.

10. The <u>women</u> and men solved the problem.

B Write the plural form of the noun in ( ).

1. At camp, the girls have busy (life).
2. They teach the younger (child) songs.
3. They help the (woman) clean the cabins.
4. They help the (man) clean the pool.
5. They rake (leaf).
6. They chase the (mouse) from the tent.
7. They feed the (goose) by the lake.
8. They brush the (ox) in the barn.
9. They look quietly at the (deer).
10. Their (foot) hurt at the end of the day.
11. They brush their (tooth) and go to bed.
12. The girls don't need to count (sheep)!

C Write sentences using the plural forms of both nouns.

13. goose, foot
14. child, woman
15. ox, tooth
16. leaf, mouse
17. man, life
18. deer, sheep

Test Preparation

 Write the letter of the plural form of each underlined noun.

1. The <u>woman</u> have a class.

   A woman   **C** womanes
   B womans   **D** women

2. They teach <u>child</u> about clean rooms.

   A childs   **C** childrens
   B children   **D** childrens'

3. Don't put your <u>foot</u> on your bed.

   A foot   **C** feet
   B foots   **D** feets

4. Put the toothpaste away after brushing your <u>tooth</u>.

   A tooth   **C** tooths
   B teeth   **D** teeths

5. Put away your toy army <u>man</u>.

   A men   **C** mens
   B man   **D** mans

6. Crumbs under the bed attract <u>mouse</u>.

   A mouse   **C** mice
   B mouses   **D** mices

7. Wipe mud and <u>leaf</u> off your shoes.

   A leafs   **C** leaves
   B leaf   **D** leafs'

8. You'll remember these rules all your <u>life</u>.

   A lives   **C** life
   B lifes   **D** life's

Review

✓ Write *S* if the underlined noun is singular. Write *P* if the underlined noun is plural.

1. The <u>children</u> saw unusual animals at the farm.
2. The <u>oxen</u> had huge heads and backs.
3. Some <u>geese</u> honked by a pond.
4. A baby <u>deer</u> had big brown eyes.
5. There were ten <u>sheep</u> with curly fur.
6. A tiny <u>mouse</u> scampered through the barn.
7. A horse with big <u>teeth</u> chewed on hay.
8. Many <u>mice</u> live in the hay.
9. The <u>woman</u> asked which animal they liked best.
10. No <u>child</u> could choose a favorite.
11. They had never seen so many cute animals in their <u>lives</u>.
12. One <u>goose</u> followed them to the car.

✓ Write the plural form of the noun in ( ).

13. The (man) solved animals' problems.
14. The Kellys wanted the (mouse) out of their house.
15. Mr. Cox wanted a fence around his (sheep).
16. A farmer didn't want (deer) in his fields.
17. The Steins said there were too many (goose).
18. Mrs. Henry's (ox) needed a bigger barn.
19. The Clydes' cat could not chew with its (tooth).
20. Bill's guinea pig would not eat its lettuce (leaf).

Writing Clearly

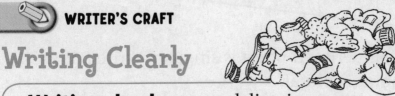

Writing clearly means delivering your message so that readers easily understand it.

Unclear	My problem was all the stuff in my closet, and it made me late.
Clear	I had extra clothes, toys, and shoes in my closet. I couldn't find what I needed, so I was late.

Follow these steps to write clearly:

- Use specific, precise words instead of vague or general ones.
- Use words such as *so* and *because* that show how ideas are related.
- Make sure words such as *it* and *they* clearly refer to specific persons or things.

Rewrite each sentence to make it clearer.

1. I like piano lessons better than soccer, and I do it twice a week.

2. We need money because the fields and uniforms are old, and they are full of weeds.

3. The firefighters talk to kids about fire prevention, and they know how to do it.

Write a sentence about a problem you have solved in school. Make sure the sentence states your meaning clearly.

Problem-Solution

A **problem-solution** paragraph describes a problem. Then it tells how the problem was solved or how it could be solved.

First part of paragraph describes problem.

Second part of paragraph describes solution. *So* signals change. *First, next,* and *finally* tell order of steps.

Conclusion tells how solution helped writer and looks to future.

My Closet Problem

My closet was a mess! I couldn't find anything in it. I was late for school three times because I couldn't find a matching pair of shoes. Toys, games, shoes, t-shirts, pants, and jackets were jumbled together on the floor and on the shelves. So I called the best organizer I know: my cousin Beth. First, we took everything out of the closet. We gave away all my old clothes. Next, we hung the rest of my clothes on the racks. I put each pair of shoes together on the shelves. Finally, we sorted all my toys and games. I put my skateboard, tennis racket, and baseball bat in the garage. I stacked up all my board games. I put my books on the shelves over my desk. Now I can actually see what I have! From now on, I am keeping my closet neat. I don't want to have to solve this problem again!

Singular Possessive Nouns

To show that one person, animal, or thing owns something, use a **singular possessive noun**. Add an apostrophe (') and the letter *s* to a singular noun to make it possessive.

Singular Noun The <u>bear</u> slept all day.

Singular Possessive Noun The hare did not like the <u>bear's</u> laziness.

A Write the possessive noun in each sentence.

1. The class talked about each person's favorite vegetable.
2. Edward likes the carrot's bright color.
3. Olivia likes broccoli's leafy tops.
4. Terrell likes his mom's bean soup.
5. Everyone enjoys the farm's good foods.
6. The farmer's stand has the freshest vegetables.
7. The corn's sweet flavor makes that soup delicious.
8. What vegetable will be good with tonight's dinner?
9. The cook's recipes for potatoes are wonderful.
10. Tracy's favorite salad includes lettuce and celery.
11. The most important thing is a vegetable's freshness.
12. I can almost taste my dad's homemade squash casserole.

B Write the singular possessive form of the underlined noun in each sentence.

1. The <u>cat</u> best friend was a pig.

2. The cat visited the <u>pig</u> home each day.

3. The pig rolled around in <u>Farmer Gray</u> muddy yard.

4. The cat couldn't believe his <u>friend</u> habit.

5. The cat was the <u>county</u> cleanest animal.

6. One day the friends surprised the <u>barnyard</u> other animals.

7. The cat rolled in the <u>hog</u> mud, and the pig stayed clean.

8. The <u>farmer</u> wife laughed at the sight of the cat.

9. I like that <u>story</u> ending.

10. The <u>teacher</u> class thought it was funny.

C Write sentences about events that might happen on a farm. Use the singular possessive form of each noun shown.

11. horse

12. cow

13. barn

14. worker

15. field

16. tractor

17. hen

18. house

Test Preparation

 Write the letter of the correct possessive noun to complete each sentence.

1. A ___ work never ends.

   A farmer

   B farmers

   C farmer's

   D farmers's

2. The ___ work begins at sunrise.

   A day

   B day's

   C days

   D days's

3. The ___ call awakens everyone.

   A rooster's

   B roosters

   C rosters's

   D rooster'

4. The ___ milk is warm.

   A cows's

   B cows

   C cow's

   D cowses

5. The farmer puts the ___ eggs in a basket.

   A hen

   B hens

   C hens's

   D hen's

6. The ___ crop is picked.

   A cornfields

   B cornfield's

   C cornfields's

   D cornfield

Review

☑ Write the possessive noun in each sentence.

1. Each farm's crops are used for different things.
2. Mr. Johnson's fields grow food crops.
3. This field's crop is potatoes.
4. Animal feed grows in Mrs. Long's fields.
5. That animal's favorite crop is grass.
6. Some of our country's crops are used for cloth.
7. Cloth is made from cotton's fibers.
8. Flowers for decorations grow on Ms. Ross's farm.
9. The meadow's wildflowers should not be picked.
10. Ms. Ross likes that rose's color best.

☑ Write the possessive form of the underlined noun in each sentence.

11. Mr. Dean day was not going well.
12. One of the tractor tires was flat.
13. A cow leg got stuck in a fence.
14. The chicken coop door was broken.
15. The dog bark scared the animals.
16. The truck engine wouldn't start.
17. Some of the roof shingles are missing.
18. The porch light has burned out.
19. The garden plants need water.
20. It was a typical farmer day.

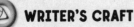

Know Your Purpose

The **purpose** of an article or story is the writer's reason for writing it. A writer's purpose may be to inform, to persuade, or to entertain readers. Knowing your purpose helps you make choices about voice, word choice, and organization.

Here are some kinds of writing that could be done for each purpose:

To inform: newspaper article, how-to article, compare and contrast essay, research report

To entertain: personal narrative, feature article, story, poem

To persuade: editorial, letter to the editor, ad

Read each paragraph. Write whether its purpose is *to inform, to entertain,* or *to persuade* readers.

1. Everyone should sign up for the park clean-up day next weekend. No one likes a park full of litter. The park is for everyone to enjoy, so everyone should help keep it beautiful.

2. A fox played a trick. She told the raccoon there were delicious apples under the maple tree. He just had to clear away the fallen leaves. The raccoon raked leaves all day with his paws. But there were no apples. "Thanks," said the fox. Then she disappeared into the cozy hole that the raccoon had uncovered for her.

Feature Story

A **feature story** tells about something interesting that happened to real people. It usually appears in a magazine or newspaper to entertain or inform readers.

Introduction gets readers' attention.

Informal language helps author accomplish purpose.

Direct quotes add interest.

Conclusion lets readers know how Jay's experience changed him.

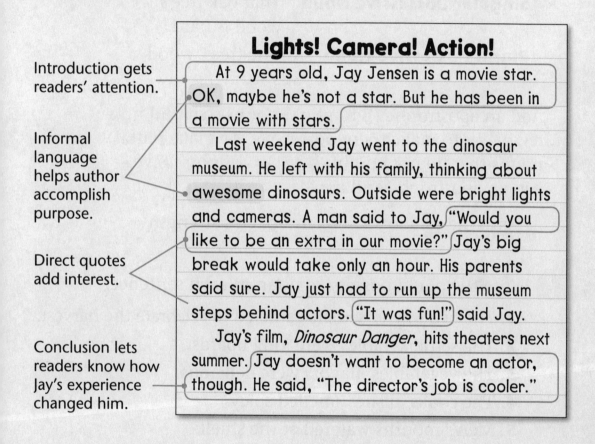

Lights! Camera! Action!

At 9 years old, Jay Jensen is a movie star. OK, maybe he's not a star. But he has been in a movie with stars.

Last weekend Jay went to the dinosaur museum. He left with his family, thinking about awesome dinosaurs. Outside were bright lights and cameras. A man said to Jay, "Would you like to be an extra in our movie?" Jay's big break would take only an hour. His parents said sure. Jay just had to run up the museum steps behind actors. "It was fun!" said Jay.

Jay's film, *Dinosaur Danger*, hits theaters next summer. Jay doesn't want to become an actor, though. He said, "The director's job is cooler."

Plural Possessive Nouns

To show that two or more people share or own something, use a **plural possessive noun**.

Plural Noun   The <u>trees</u> grew tall in America.

Singular Possessive Noun   That oak <u>tree's</u> wood is hard.

Plural Possessive Noun   All the <u>trees'</u> wood was strong.

Add an apostrophe (') to plural nouns that end in *-s*, *-es*, or *-ies* to make them possessive. To make plural nouns that do not end in *-s, -es, or -ies* possessive, add an apostrophe and an *s*.

<u>men</u>   <u>men's</u> boots   <u>oxen</u>   <u>oxen's</u> strength

A Write the plural possessive noun in each sentence.

1. The two towns' settlers gathered to celebrate the harvest.

2. The settlers' tables were long boards.

3. The vegetables' flavors were delicious.

4. The cooks' dishes smelled spicy.

5. Men's mouths watered at the smell.

6. The colonies' schools taught reading and arithmetic.

7. Americans' roads were dusty paths.

8. Horses pulled farmers' carts and wagons.

9. The horses' jobs were difficult.

10. Oxen's size made them a better choice for the job.

B Write the possessive form of the underlined plural noun in each sentence.

1. Most <u>countries</u> houses have different styles.
2. Some <u>Africans</u> homes are mud huts.
3. In England, <u>occupants</u> houses may be very old.
4. <u>Mexicans</u> houses are made to be cool.
5. <u>Canadians</u> houses must stay warm.
6. Coastal <u>residents</u> homes might be on stilts.
7. <u>Islanders</u> houses must stand up to wind and rain.
8. Some <u>Native Americans</u> homes could be moved from place to place.
9. Some <u>renters</u> apartments are in tall buildings.
10. Are <u>Eskimos</u> houses really made of ice?
11. Some <u>sailors</u> homes are their boats.
12. <u>Builders</u> challenges are different in every place.

C Write sentences about different kinds of houses in different places. Use the plural possessive form of each noun in your sentence.

13. roof
14. city
15. lawn
16. neighborhood
17. family
18. children

Test Preparation

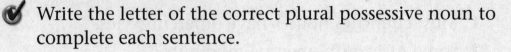 Write the letter of the correct plural possessive noun to complete each sentence.

1. Many ___ efforts are needed to build a house.

   A individuals

   B individuals'

   C individuals's

   D individual's

2. The two ___ plans are on the table.

   A designer's

   B designers

   C designers'

   D designers's

3. All the ___ designs are unusual.

   A room's

   B rooms'

   C rooms's

   D rooms

4. The three ___ tools are in a truck.

   A carpenter's

   B carpenters's

   C carpenters

   D carpenters'

5. The ___ days are hard and busy.

   A men's

   B mens'

   C mens

   D men

6. The three ___ talents make the house beautiful.

   A painters

   B painters'

   C painters's

   D painter's

Review

☑ Write the plural possessive noun in each sentence.

1. The colonies' first settlers came from England on ships.

2. The ships' passengers wanted to get rich.

3. The passengers' journey was long and hard.

4. The men's first settlement was in Jamestown.

5. The settlers' hardships almost led to disaster.

6. Captain John Smith's leadership raised the newcomers' spirits.

☑ Write the possessive form of the underlined plural noun in each sentence.

7. The <u>colonists</u> laziness caused some problems.

8. The nearby <u>Indians</u> leader was Powhatan.

9. The two <u>groups</u> goal was to get along with one another.

10. Most <u>settlements</u> farms soon produced crops.

11. The <u>women</u> arrival helped the settlements succeed.

12. Fires destroyed many <u>folks</u> homes in the late 1600s.

13. The <u>Virginians</u> new home was Williamsburg.

14. Both <u>towns</u> histories are fascinating.

15. Many <u>buildings</u> ruins still stand in Jamestown.

16. They teach us about <u>Americans</u> struggles in the past.

17. We can read the <u>leaders</u> letters and journals.

18. They tell about many <u>children</u> deaths.

Use Precise Words

Precise words tell a writer's exact meaning. For example, the words *hut, shack, lodge, cabin,* and *mansion* give readers a better picture than *house.* Using precise words can also help you use fewer words.

Wordy	The cow <u>made a loud, angry sound</u>.
Precise	The cow <u>bellowed</u>.

 Write the sentences. Replace the underlined words with one precise word.

1. The girls <u>laughed in a high, happy, breathless way</u>.

2. John and Holly <u>walked in a slow and relaxed way</u> around the mall.

3. The pig <u>made a sharp, shrill noise</u>.

4. Suddenly a child <u>let out a loud, piercing cry</u>.

5. Across the street from the cabin was a <u>body of water that was smaller and calmer than a lake</u>.

6. For the holiday, the family had a <u>big meal with many different dishes</u>.

Write several sentences about an animal. Use precise words to tell about things the animal does.

Writing for Tests

Prompt Suppose you are introducing a new student to your school. What <u>important facts about your school</u> would you explain to him or her? Write an <u>explanatory paragraph</u> to a <u>new student</u> telling what he or she should know.

Topic sentence that tells what the paragraph is about.

Words and phrases show the order of events during the day.

Conclusion shows that the paragraph is finished.

Life at McKinley School

The third-grade class at McKinley School is a great place to learn! At 9:00 each morning Mr. Chase, the principal, makes announcements. Then third graders have reading and spelling. At noon, we go to lunch. All the classes' lunch periods are at different times. You can bring your lunch, or you can buy it. (On Wednesdays, the lunchroom serves spaghetti. It's great!) After lunch we have social studies and then physical education. Then we have math and science. In late afternoon, we work on projects, such as the science fair. Sometimes we have a field trip, like to the art museum. Finally, Ms. Perez reviews our homework assignments. It's the end of another educational day at McKinley School.

Action and Linking Verbs

A **verb** is a word that tells what someone or something is or does. **Action verbs** are words that show action. **Linking verbs,** such as *am, is, are, was,* and *were,* do not show action. They link a subject to a word or words in the predicate.

Action Verb Roses <u>grow</u> on bushes in the garden. They <u>have</u> soft petals.

Linking Verb Each rose <u>is</u> a different color.

Ⓐ Write the verb in each sentence.

1. We see many wildflowers on our trips.
2. Wildflowers have wonderful names.
3. My favorites are bluebonnets.
4. Queen Anne's Lace is a soft white flower.
5. My sister loves little yellow buttercups.
6. Wildflowers wilt on a hot day.
7. Once I picked a fairy slipper.
8. Clover is usually purple.
9. Tina steps on a lily by mistake.
10. Forests are full of violets and other wildflowers.

B Write the verb in each sentence. Write *A* after an action verb. Write *L* after a linking verb.

1. Some flowers grow from bulbs.
2. A bulb is an underground stem.
3. Gardeners plant some bulbs in the fall.
4. Tulips come from bulbs.
5. Flowers from bulbs bloom each year.
6. Other flowers start as seeds.
7. They are annuals.
8. My favorite annual is a snapdragon.
9. It has many little blossoms.
10. Petunias are annuals also.

C Add a verb to complete each sentence. Write the sentence.

11. A garden ___ a peaceful place to relax.
12. Butterflies ___ around the flowers.
13. Leaves ___ in the breeze.
14. The flowers ___ colorful and fragrant.
15. Bees ___ noisily around the flowers and vegetables.

Test Preparation

 Write the letter of the word that is a verb.

1. You find flowers in many places.

   A find

   B in

   C many

   D flowers

2. Poppies bloom in the desert.

   A Poppies

   B bloom

   C in

   D desert

3. A cactus has pretty flowers.

   A cactus

   B has

   C pretty

   D flowers

4. Many plants are in the mountains.

   A plants

   B Many

   C mountains

   D are

5. A sunflower grows on the prairie.

   A sunflower

   B prairie

   C grows

   D on

6. Water lilies live in the forest.

   A Water

   B lilies

   C live

   D forest

Review

✓ Write the verb in each sentence.

1. Alex wants vegetables in his garden.

2. He plants many different seeds.

3. He waters the plants each day.

4. The garden is soon full of vegetables.

5. Carrots are Alex's favorite vegetable.

6. The carrots have bushy green tops.

7. Rabbits like the carrot plants.

8. Those plants are tomatoes.

9. Alex weeds the garden often.

10. The garden is a big success.

✓ Write the verb in each sentence. Write *A* after an action verb. Write *L* after a linking verb.

11. Herbs bloom in Shawna's garden.

12. Parsley and rosemary are herbs.

13. The garden has mint and sage too.

14. Shawna's mom cooks with the herbs.

15. She puts parsley in the soup.

16. The parsley is fresh and green.

17. Shawna saves the mint for tea.

18. The mint is cool and spicy.

19. Shawna tastes sage in the chicken.

20. The herbs are delicious.

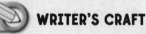

Sensory Details

> **Sensory details** describe the way something looks, sounds, feels, tastes, or smells.
>
> **Sight** The baked chicken was golden brown.
>
> **Sound** Juices in the pan were hissing and popping.
>
> **Smell** The sauce smelled like ripe plums.
>
> **Taste** I bit into the warm, tender meat.
>
> **Touch** The sauce made my fingers sticky.

Read each description. Write whether it appeals mainly to the sense of *sight, sound, smell, taste,* or *touch.*

1. The air is perfumed with the sweetness of roses in bloom and recently mown grass.

2. I am awakened by the soft chirps of robins, the loud honks of geese, and the rowdy cries of crows.

3. The moon is a big golden pumpkin in the autumn sky.

4. The chill stings my nose and hands and creeps under my coat.

5. I love salty pretzels dipped in mustard sauce.

6. A siren screamed through the darkness.

Write three sentences. Each sentence should appeal to a different sense.

Journal Entry

A person writes a **journal entry** to describe an idea, feeling, or experience he or she has had.

First sentence tells what the entry is about.

Color words create details that appeal to the sense of sight.

Vivid words create sensory details.

Comparison creates a vivid sensory detail.

My Favorite Place

I love the beach on a summer day. I see white sand, dark blue water, and light blue sky. The sea gulls make sharp cries overhead, and the ocean roars in the background. I smell the salty air and suntan lotion on the people around me. The sand feels warm and scratchy under my bare feet, and the ocean breeze feels fresh on my face. When I finally get the nerve to go in the water, it feels like ice, and the waves startle me. But then I get used to it. The water feels refreshing, and the waves have a nice rhythm. The beach is my favorite place.

Main and Helping Verbs

A **verb phrase** is a verb that has more than one word. The **main verb** shows action. A **helping verb** shows the time of the action. In the following sentence, *telling* is the main verb, and *are* is the helping verb.

The people are telling stories.

The helping verbs *am, is,* and *are* show present time. *Was* and *were* show past time. *Will* shows future time. The helping verbs *has, have,* and *had* show that an action happened in the past. In the following sentences, *had* and *will* are helping verbs.

He had told that story before. He will tell that story again.

A Write the verb phrase in each sentence.

1. The Native Americans had told interesting legends.

2. They were explaining the world around them.

3. I have heard legends about the sun and the moon.

4. In some stories, animals are talking like people.

5. Someday I will entertain you with the stories.

6. I am writing a legend.

7. I have set the story in a forest.

8. The flowers are talking to the trees.

9. The huge trees will care for the little flowers.

10. You will hear my story soon.

B Look at the underlined verb in each sentence. Write *M* if it is a main verb. Write *H* if it is a helping verb.

1. Those Native Americans were <u>living</u> in a rich region.
2. The land <u>was</u> covered with trees.
3. The women are <u>picking</u> berries.
4. The men <u>are</u> gathering for a feast.
5. The host <u>will</u> serve good food.
6. The people had <u>created</u> beautiful copper shields.
7. They <u>were</u> fishing for salmon.
8. Some boys were <u>cutting</u> redwood trees.
9. They <u>have</u> painted colorful designs on the wood.
10. Their canoes will <u>hold</u> many men.
11. The men are <u>paddling</u> the canoes up the river.
12. One woman <u>has</u> found some wild blueberries.

C Add a verb phrase with a main verb and a helping verb to complete each sentence. Write the sentence.

13. People in the village ___ their resources wisely.
14. They ___ homes and canoes from wood.
15. The people ___ fish from the ocean.
16. Men and boys ___ deer and moose in the woods.
17. Craftspeople ___ beautiful blankets and masks.
18. Villagers always ___ the land and the ocean.

Test Preparation

 Write the letter that shows the main verb in each sentence.

1. The villagers had held a festival.

   A had

   B had held

   C villagers had

   D held

2. They were celebrating a good harvest.

   A were

   B celebrating

   C were celebrating

   D they

3. They have danced around a campfire.

   A have

   B have danced

   C danced

   D around

4. They are eating a delicious feast.

   A They

   B are

   C eating

   D feast

5. They will have another festival next year.

   A have

   B will have

   C will

   D They

6. My grandparents had attended the festival several years ago.

   A had attended

   B attended

   C had

   D My

Review

✓ Write the verb phrase in each sentence.

1. The Native Americans on the plains were hunting buffalo.
2. The hunters are wearing deerskin leggings.
3. The women had planted squash.
4. They will grind corn for cornmeal.
5. The children are sleeping in a log lodge.
6. Other Indians were living in the Southwest.
7. They had built homes of adobe bricks.
8. The girls have displayed their dolls.
9. The boys are rolling a hoop.
10. The children will play all day.

✓ Look at the underlined verb in each sentence. Write *M* if it is a main verb. Write *H* if it is a helping verb.

11. The Pueblo people had <u>woven</u> beautiful cloth.
12. They <u>have</u> shaped pottery.
13. The artists <u>are</u> painting the pots with colorful designs.
14. The Navajo were <u>stitching</u> colorful blankets.
15. They are <u>creating</u> silver jewelry.
16. The Pomo people <u>were</u> making baskets.
17. They <u>had</u> decorated them with feathers.
18. The baskets <u>will</u> hold water.
19. That drum was <u>crafted</u> by an Arapaho.
20. Who was <u>wearing</u> that beaded belt?

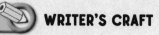

Strong Verbs

> **Strong verbs** are verbs that describe an action precisely. Here are some strong verbs that might be used in place of *run:*
>
> scramble   rush   sprint   gallop   trot

Write each sentence. Replace the underlined verb with a verb that is more vivid and precise. You may need to add or take out other words.

1. The coyote <u>walked</u> slyly toward the people.

2. The coyote <u>laughed</u> at his trick.

3. The other animals <u>spoke</u> to the coyote.

4. The coyote <u>talked</u> about how smart he was.

5. The lazy coyote <u>lay</u> against a tree.

6. The coyote <u>took</u> a nap in the warm sun.

7. When he woke up, he <u>wanted</u> food.

8. The other animals <u>said</u> that he should find his own food.

Write a sentence about a tricky coyote or another clever animal. Use a strong verb.

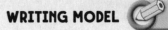

Skit

> A **skit** is a short play with a few characters. The plot, or events, of a skit are told through dialogue. Dialogue consists of the words the characters say to one another.

How Coyote Stole Fire

NARRATOR: Long ago, people had no fire.

A character explains the problem.

COYOTE: People get cold in winter. The Fire Beings have fire. But they will not share it. I will go take it.

NARRATOR: Coyote went into the hills. He spied on the Fire Beings, but they guarded fire all the time. They didn't want others to have it.

Skits are often read and not performed. Strong verbs help readers picture the action in their minds.

COYOTE: *(He hides behind a tree.)* I have been here all day. Now it is late at night. The Fire Being who is guarding the fire is asleep. *(He grabs fire from the Fire Being and runs; the Fire Being chases him. The fire passes from Coyote to Beaver, Squirrel, and Chipmunk; all are chased by Fire Being. The fire is passed to Tree, and Fire Being cannot get it. Fire Being leaves.)*

Narrator provides the conclusion.

NARRATOR: I will show how to get fire from Tree. *(Rubbing two branches together, he starts a fire. The people look happy.)*

Subject-Verb Agreement

The subject and the verb in a sentence must work together, or **agree**.

To make most present tense verbs agree with singular nouns or *he, she,* or *it,* add -*s*. If the subject is a plural noun or *I, you, we,* or *they,* the present tense verb does not end in -*s*.

Singular Subject	The <u>sun</u> <u>sets</u> today.
Plural Subject	The <u>girls</u> <u>play</u> outside.
Plural Subject	<u>A boy and a dog</u> <u>sit</u> there.

A form of *be* in a sentence also must agree with the subject. Use *is* or *was* to agree with singular nouns. Use *are* or *were* to agree with plural nouns.

Singular Subject	The <u>moon</u> <u>is shining</u> brightly. The <u>moon</u> <u>is</u> full.
Plural Subject	<u>Fireflies</u> <u>are lighting</u> the sky. <u>They</u> <u>were</u> everywhere.

A Write *C* next to each sentence that is correct.

1. Two deer is standing in the clearing.
2. David steps on a branch.
3. Both deer scampers away.
4. Their white tails lift like flags.
5. These animals are graceful.

B Choose the verb in ( ) that agrees with the subject. Write the sentence.

1. Some animals (stay, stays) awake at night.

2. Bats (is, are) flying around the treetops.

3. Raccoons (are, is) prowling in the yard.

4. In the wild, a wolf (howl, howls).

5. An owl (hoot, hoots) in the forest.

6. Beavers (works, work) at night.

7. A moth and a firefly (is, are) fluttering in the dark.

8. The neighbors' cat (cry, cries) out at midnight.

9. A bullfrog (is, are) croaking at the pond.

10. Many animals (is, are) night creatures.

C Write sentences. Use each numbered phrase as a subject, along with a verb from the box. Make each verb agree with its subject. You may use the same verb more than once.

bark	spin	crawl	sway	glow

11. The stars and the moon

12. A little snake

13. A neighborhood dog

14. The tree branches

15. A spider

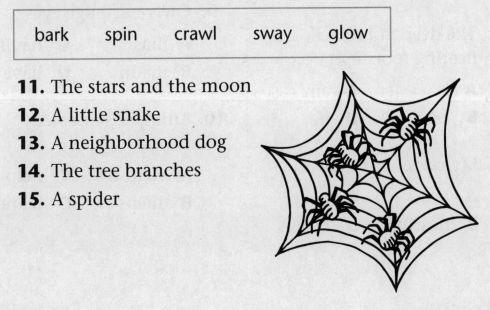

Test Preparation

 Write the letter of the verb that completes each sentence.

1. Animals ___ all their senses at night.

   A uses   **C** useing

   B using   **D** use

2. Some animals ___ well in the dark.

   A seen   **C** see

   B seeing   **D** sees

3. Wolves ___ other animals.

   A smelling   **C** smells

   B smell   **D** smelles

4. The deer and the elk ___ hearing footsteps.

   A is   **C** am

   B are   **D** be

5. My cat ___ tiny insects.

   A hears   **C** hear

   B hearing   **D** heares

6. The cat ___ using its bright eyes also.

   A are   **C** was

   B am   **D** were

7. A raccoon ___ for food.

   A sniff   **C** sniffing

   B sniffs   **D** sniffs'

8. The bats ___ hearing echoes.

   A are   **C** is

   B was   **D** am

9. Owls ___ huge eyes.

   A has   **C** having

   B hadnt   **D** have

10. Animals' senses ___ them.

    A helping   **C** help

    B helps   **D** helpes

Review

✓ Write the sentence from each pair that is correct.

1. The girls is camping in the woods.
   The girls are camping in the woods.

2. The campers hear many sounds.
   The campers hears many sounds.

3. Some birds call at night.
   Some birds calls at night.

4. A small animal is scampering in the bushes.
   A small animal are scampering in the bushes.

5. Coyotes was howling in the distance.
   Coyotes were howling in the distance.

✓ Choose the verb in ( ) that agrees with the subject. Write the sentence.

6. The desert (is, are) alive at night.

7. Desert animals (sleep, sleeps) during the hot day.

8. Snakes (slither, slithers) out of holes at night.

9. Mice (runs, run) across the dry ground.

10. A fox (is, are) looking for food.

11. Jackrabbits (hop, hops) around the cactus.

12. Two little rats (was, were) hiding from the wolves.

13. A lizard and a toad (is, are) sitting under a rock.

14. A big owl (watch, watches) the animals.

15. A cool breeze (blow, blows) through the desert.

Putting Ideas in Order

You can **put your ideas in order** in several different ways:

- To describe an event, use time order.
- To describe a place or a thing, use space order. For example, go from top to bottom or from left to right.
- To compare and contrast two things, describe their likenesses. Then describe their differences.
- To explain causes and effects, describe the causes. Then explain the effects of the causes.

Read the paragraph. Write whether the paragraph is in *time order, space order, comparison-contrast order,* or *cause-effect order.*

Garden flowers and wildflowers are both beautiful and colorful. However, garden flowers grow in small areas. They need to be weeded and watered by people. On the other hand, wildflowers often grow in big fields or forests. They just need sunlight and rain to keep growing.

Write a short description of a place. Use space order.

Friendly Letter

A **friendly letter** is written by a person to a friend or family member. The letter expresses the writer's experiences and feelings. A friendly letter begins with a greeting and ends with a closing.

First sentence tells what the topic is.

Writer describes events in sequence.

Writer uses time-order words and vivid descriptive words.

Last sentence sums up letter. Closing indicates friendly letter.

A Thunderstorm

July 2, _____

Dear Luisa,

We had the most amazing storm yesterday! It was much worse than the one we had at camp last year. It was a hot, muggy afternoon, and I was reading a book on our porch. Suddenly black clouds formed in the sky. I saw a zigzag of lightning. Soon I heard a loud crash of thunder, and I ran inside. A few fat raindrops fell on the porch. Before long, rain was pouring out of the sky. The wind battered the trees and bushes. The downpour went on for ten minutes.

Then suddenly the storm ended. In another ten minutes, the sun reappeared. Soon the only signs of the storm were the puddles on my porch. I know you love nature, so I just had to tell you about this awesome summer storm.

Your friend,
Maya

Present, Past, and Future Tenses

Verbs can show when an action happens. This is called **tense**. Different verb tenses have different forms. Many present tense verbs end in -*s*. Form the past tense of many verbs by adding -*ed*. Add the helping verb *will* to a verb to show future tense.

Present Tense   A fish <u>jumps</u> out of the pond.

Past Tense   The boy <u>pulled</u> the fish in on a line.

Future Tense   The boy <u>will toss</u> the fish back.

- When a verb ends with *e*, drop the *e* before adding -*ed: close closed*

- When a one-syllable verb ends with one vowel followed by one consonant, double the final consonant before adding -*ed: hop hopped*

- When a verb ends with a consonant followed by *y*, change the *y* to *i* before adding -*ed: cry cried*

A Tell the tense of the underlined verb in each sentence. Write *present, past,* or *future*.

1. A whale <u>calls</u> to other whales.

2. The whale <u>will use</u> the sound's echo.

3. A whale's tail <u>moves</u> up and down.

4. The whale <u>will glide</u> through the water.

5. The whale <u>breathed</u> through the blowhole on its head.

6. Ice <u>trapped</u> the whales in the bay.

B Choose the verb in ( ) that completes each sentence. Use the tense that follows the sentence. Write the sentence.

1. Many different kinds of whales (lived, live) in the oceans. (present)

2. The gentle waves (carry, carried) the whales with them. (past)

3. You (will discover, discovered) gray whales in the North Pacific. (future)

4. Greenland whales (will measure, measure) up to 60 feet long. (present)

5. The size of a blue whale (surprised, will surprise) you. (future)

6. The humpback whale (uses, used) long flippers. (past)

7. Many humpback whales (stay, will stay) near the coast. (future)

C Choose a verb from the word bank to complete each sentence. Use each verb in the tense shown.

collect	hurry	provide	tap	travel

8. A baby whale ___ along near its mother. (past)

9. A mother whale gently ___ her baby's body. (past)

10. Warm waters ___ a nice home for the babies. (past)

11. The whales ___ to cold waters in summer. (present)

12. They ___ much food there. (future)

Test Preparation

Write the letter of the verb that completes each sentence. Use the tense in ( ).

1. We ___ some whales off the coast. (past)

    A view

    B viewed

    C will view

    D views

2. A whale ___ its tail out of the water. (past)

    A flips

    B will flip

    C flipped

    D fliped

3. The whale ___ the water with its tail. (present)

    A slaps

    B slapping

    C slapped

    D slap

4. The whale's tail ___ very loud. (future)

    A sound

    B sounded

    C will sound

    D sounding

5. Sometimes whales ___ their heads through the water. (future)

    A will poke

    B poke

    C poking

    D pokes

6. The whales ___ with an unusual sound. (past)

    A crying

    B cried

    C cryed

    D cry

Review

✓ Tell the tense of the underlined verb in each sentence. Write *present, past,* or *future.*

1. Scientists <u>classified</u> dolphins as whales.

2. Dolphins <u>will learn</u> quickly.

3. People <u>call</u> a group of dolphins a school.

4. A school of dolphins <u>followed</u> a ship.

5. The animals <u>turn</u> flips in the ocean.

✓ Choose the verb in ( ) that completes each sentence. Use the tense that follows the sentence. Write the sentence.

6. Dolphins (performed, perform) in the show. (past)

7. They (invent, will invent) their own tricks. (future)

8. A dolphin (tosses, tossed) a ball through a hoop. (past)

9. Two dolphins (jump, will jump) over a net. (present)

10. Dolphins (produce, will produce) whistles and clicks. (future)

11. The sounds (echo, echoed) off objects in the water. (present)

12. Dolphins' good vision (helps, helped) them too. (present)

13. The ancient Greeks (liked, like) dolphins. (past)

14. The people (painted, will paint) dolphins on their pottery. (past)

15. Sailors still (consider, will consider) dolphins good luck. (present)

Answer the 5 Ws and How

> A good news story answers the questions **who, what, where, when,** and **why** about an event. It might also answer the question **how** about the event.

Read the news story. Answer the questions.

Lunch Guest

A Boulder family had an unexpected lunch guest yesterday. At approximately 12:45 P.M. Charles, Ava, and Alex Martin were eating lunch on their back deck. They suddenly remembered that Alex had soccer practice and rushed inside, leaving their uneaten food on the table. Just as they were about to leave, Mr. Martin decided to bring in the food. "I didn't want to attract any squirrels or raccoons," Mr. Martin said. "Little did I know what had already shown up." When he went outside, Mr. Martin found a huge black bear enjoying the family's chicken salad and apple pie. Mr. Martin went indoors and called the fire department. However, the bear—and the food—were gone before help arrived.

---

1. *Who* was involved in the event?

2. *What* happened?

3. *Where* did the event happen?

4. *When* did the event happen?

5. *Why* was the bear able to steal the food?

News Story

A **news story** describes an interesting recent event. It answers the questions *who, what, where, when,* and *why* about the event. These questions are called the 5 Ws. The news story often also answers the question *how* about the event.

First sentence provides an interesting lead.

News story answers the 5 Ws and *how.*

Last sentence provides a conclusion.

Saving Whales

Thousands of whales in the Northern Hemisphere owe their lives to a young girl. On April 18, a herd of whales became stranded near a shore of the Antarctic Ocean. The Edir Konek family of Pontak heard strange sounds and discovered the group of whales stuck in the bay. After discovering that the path to the ocean was covered with ice, the Koneks called an icebreaker to save the whales.

Captain George Turner and his crew arrived. Time was running out for the whales when young Glashka Konek had an idea. "I suggested the crew play music for the whales," Glashka said. "I thought it would calm the whales and get them to move." Turner's crew tried many kinds of music, but the whales would not budge. Then Captain Turner played classical music. The whales followed the boat and were saved.

Irregular Verbs

Usually you add -*ed* to a verb to show past tense.
Irregular verbs do not follow this rule. These verbs change to other words to show past tense.

Present Tense   We <u>see</u> a volcano.

Past Tense   We <u>saw</u> a volcano.

**Past with *has*,   We <u>have seen</u> a volcano.
have, or *had***

Verb	Past Tense	Past with *has, have,* or *had*
begin	began	(*has, have, had*) begun
do	did	(*has, have, had*) done
find	found	(*has, have, had*) found
give	gave	(*has, have, had*) given
go	went	(*has, have, had*) gone
run	ran	(*has, have, had*) run
see	saw	(*has, have, had*) seen
take	took	(*has, have, had*) taken
think	thought	(*has, have, had*) thought
wear	wore	(*has, have, had*) worn

A Write the correct form of the irregular verb in ( ).

    1. That island (begun, began) as a volcano.

    2. A volcano in the ocean (gone, went) off.

    3. Lava has (run, ran) into the ocean.

    4. We have (taken, took) a trip to that island.

B Write each sentence. Use the correct past form of the verb in ( ).

1. We (see) the world's largest volcano in Hawaii.

2. We had (go) to the big island of Hawaii for a vacation.

3. My uncle (take) us to Mauna Loa for the day.

4. We (find) a nice hiking trail on the volcano's slope.

5. I had (wear) a warm sweater, and I was glad.

6. The next day, we (go) to another volcano in Hawaii.

7. Kilauea (begin) erupting.

8. Bright red lava had (run) down the volcano.

9. Now I have (see) two volcanoes.

10. I (do) a report on the volcanoes after my trip.

C Use verbs from the chart to complete the sentences. Write the sentences.

11. Yesterday lava ____ down the volcano.

12. The eruption had ____ a month ago.

13. I ____ Mount St. Helens last spring.

14. The sunshine that day ____ the volcano a cheerful look.

15. I always had ____ volcanoes were scary.

Test Preparation

 Write the letter of the verb that completes each sentence.

1. We ___ many natural wonders in Hawaii.

    A finding   **C** found

    B finded   **D** founded

2. We ___ two active volcanoes.

    A saw   **C** seed

    B sawn   **D** seen

3. We had ___ to a rain forest.

    A go   **C** went

    B gone   **D** going

4. We have ___ into big ocean waves.

    A run   **C** ran

    B running **D** runned

5. Our teacher has ___ a talk about Hawaii's formation.

    A gave   **C** giving

    B give   **D** given

6. It ___ as five volcanoes.

    A begun   **C** begin

    B began   **D** beginning

7. We have ___ a tour of a pineapple farm.

    A took   **C** taken

    B taking   **D** taked

8. Katie has ___ many wonderful places.

    A saw   **C** seen

    B see   **D** seeing

Review

✓ Write the correct form of the irregular verb in ( ) to complete each sentence.

1. I (did, done) a report about a volcano in Mexico.
2. It (begun, began) in 1943.
3. Lava had (run, ran) out of a crack in a farmer's cornfield.
4. After six days, the farmer had (find, found) a 500-foot volcano in his field.
5. That must have (gave, given) him quite a scare!

✓ Write each sentence. Use the correct past form of the verb in ( ).

6. I (think) Krakatoa was an incredible volcano.
7. It (give) an unbelievable boom when it erupted in 1883.
8. The volcano (do) a great amount of damage.
9. My family has (take) a trip to Lassen Peak in California.
10. That volcano had (begin) erupting in May 1914.
11. A year later, an explosion (go) off and ruined a nearby forest.
12. We (see) strange lava formations near Lassen Peak.
13. Mount Katmai in Alaska had (go) off in 1912.
14. Lava and ash (run) for 15 miles and formed a valley.
15. I always have (find) volcanoes interesting.

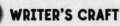

Compare/Contrast Words

When you compare or contrast two things, use words that signal how the two things are alike and different.

Alike   Spring is a warm season.
Summer is <u>also</u> warm.

Different   Spring is often rainy, <u>but</u>
summer is usually dry.

Use a word or words from the box to signal a likeness or difference in each pair of sentences. Write the sentences as two sentences or combine them into a compound sentence. Write a final sentence that compares or contrasts two insects.

and	also	as well
but	however	on the other hand

1. Leaves are green in summer. They turn red in autumn.

2. Oak trees lose their leaves in winter. Pine trees keep their leaves all year.

3. Tulips bloom in spring. Lilies bloom in spring.

4. Redwood trees grow very tall. Sequoias grow taller.

5. The plants in your garden need water every day in summer. Trees need water.

6. (Your sentence)

Writing for Tests

> **Prompt**   Think about <u>two things in nature</u>. They might be two birds, two trees, or two seasons. Write a <u>compare/contrast paragraph</u> for a nature magazine that tells how the two things are <u>alike</u> and <u>different</u>. Use <u>compare/contrast words</u> to signal similarities and differences.

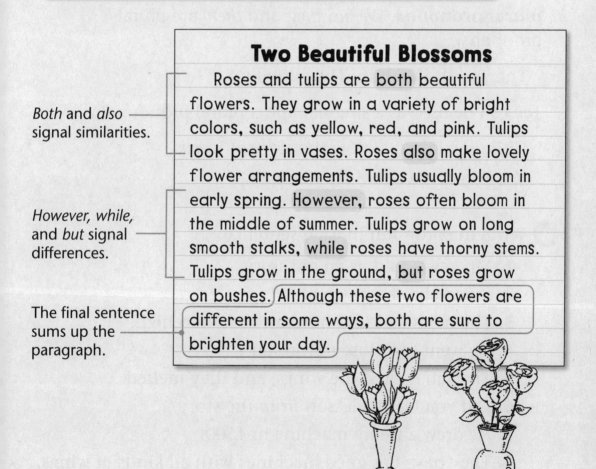

Two Beautiful Blossoms

Both and *also* signal similarities.

Roses and tulips are both beautiful flowers. They grow in a variety of bright colors, such as yellow, red, and pink. Tulips look pretty in vases. Roses also make lovely flower arrangements. Tulips usually bloom in early spring.

However, while, and *but* signal differences.

However, roses often bloom in the middle of summer. Tulips grow on long smooth stalks, while roses have thorny stems. Tulips grow in the ground, but roses grow on bushes.

The final sentence sums up the paragraph.

Although these two flowers are different in some ways, both are sure to brighten your day.

Singular and Plural Pronouns

Pronouns are words that take the place of nouns. Pronouns that take the place of singular nouns are **singular pronouns**. *I, me, he, she, him, her,* and *it* are singular pronouns.

The <u>plane</u> took off. <u>It</u> took off.

Pronouns that take the place of plural nouns are **plural pronouns**. *We, us, they,* and *them* are plural pronouns.

The <u>wheels</u> lifted up. <u>They</u> lifted up.

You can be used as a singular and a plural pronoun.

<u>Children</u>, do <u>you</u> know the story of Icarus?
<u>Icarus</u>, <u>you</u> must not fly too high.

A Write the pronoun in each sentence.

1. Mr. Lewis told us an old story.

2. It was about a boy with wings.

3. The boy's dad told him not to fly too high.

4. He went too close to the sun.

5. The sun heated the wings, and they melted.

6. Did you learn a lesson from the story?

7. He drew a flying machine in 1500.

8. They have designed machines with all kinds of wings.

B Write *S* if the underlined pronoun is singular. Write *P* if it is plural.

1. Orville Wright and <u>he</u> built the first successful airplane over a century ago.

2. <u>They</u> flew the plane in 1903.

3. A woman watched from afar, and <u>she</u> was amazed.

4. Louis Bleriot built a plane and flew <u>it</u> from France to England.

5. Early planes were unlike those that carry <u>us</u>.

6. Ben, <u>you</u> would like the Wright brothers' glider.

7. <u>It</u> had two wings, one atop the other.

8. Companies held air races and from <u>them</u> developed better airplanes.

9. <u>I</u> am interested in old airplanes.

C Revise each pair of sentences. Replace the underlined words with one of these pronouns: *she, he, they.*

10. The government sold planes from World War I. <u>The planes</u> were made of wood and cloth.

11. Charles Lindbergh flew nonstop across the Atlantic Ocean. <u>Lindbergh</u> was the first to do this alone.

12. Amelia Earhart flew across the Atlantic Ocean nonstop. <u>Earhart</u> flew in a plane called *Friendship*.

Test Preparation

 Write the letter of the pronoun that can replace the underlined word or words.

1. <u>People</u> were fascinated by flying.

A He   **C** They

B She   **D** I

2. A four-engine plane was flown by <u>a Russian inventor</u>.

A we   **C** them

B him   **D** you

3. <u>Richard Byrd</u> flew across the North Pole.

A They   **C** We

B She   **D** He

4. <u>Lindbergh's plane</u> was the *Spirit of St. Louis*.

A It   **C** They

B He   **D** Them

5. <u>Herndon and Pangborn</u> flew across the Pacific.

A We   **C** They

B He   **D** Us

6. <u>Amelia Earhart</u> tried to fly around the world.

A He   **C** They

B She   **D** Us

7. Many speed records were set by <u>Jacqueline Cochran</u>.

A us   **C** her

B them   **D** me

8. Courage was needed in <u>early flights</u>.

A them   **C** him

B it   **D** her

Review

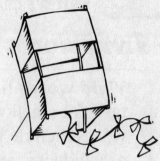

✓ Write the pronoun in each sentence.

1. We flew a kite outside.

2. It was in the shape of a box.

3. Dad and I made the kite carefully.

4. The wind was blowing all around us.

5. Dad let the kite go, and it soared above the trees.

6. Darcy came along, and she wanted to hold the kite.

7. Dad handed the string to her.

8. Tyler was there, and Darcy handed the string to him.

9. They ran around the field with the kite.

10. The kite entertained them all afternoon.

✓ Write *S* if the underlined pronoun is singular. Write *P* if it is plural.

11. Students, did <u>you</u> know that a kite is an aircraft?

12. The Chinese made <u>them</u> thousands of years ago.

13. Benjamin Franklin made a kite and flew <u>it</u> during a storm.

14. <u>He</u> learned about electricity from the kite.

15. The Wright brothers made kites and studied <u>them</u>.

16. <u>They</u> learned about wings from the kites.

17. Lorraine's father gives <u>her</u> a new kite every spring.

18. <u>We</u> can make our own kites.

19. Joanna is an artist, and <u>she</u> builds beautiful kites.

20. <u>I</u> like kites because they are fun.

Vivid Words

> **Vivid words** help readers see, hear, touch, taste, or smell what the writer describes. Vivid words include verbs such as *swirl,* nouns such as *whirlwind,* and adjectives such as *slick.*

Replace the underlined word or words with a more vivid word from the box or your own word.

fierce	crashed	clutched	howled	fluttered
wailed	whispered	fluffy	ripped	stroked

1. The breeze blew <u>full</u> clouds across the sky.

2. Trees' leaves <u>moved</u> in the breeze.

3. Suddenly the wind became <u>bad</u>.

4. It <u>took</u> the petals off the wildflowers.

5. The wind <u>made a big noise</u> through the trees.

6. A tree limb <u>fell</u> against the house.

7. The little boy <u>cried</u> and <u>held</u> his mother.

8. She <u>touched</u> his hair and <u>talked</u> to him.

Write a sentence about how the wind moves. Use two vivid words. Underline them.

Poem

A **poem** uses vivid words to describe a person, place, thing, event, or feeling. A poem has many or all of these characteristics.

- Words are arranged in *lines*. Each line may be a complete sentence or a group of words that makes sense.
- Words are used in fresh ways to create pictures, or images.
- Lines may be arranged in groups called *stanzas*.
- Some lines may *rhyme*. This means that the ending sounds of two words are the same.
- The lines have *rhythm*. Their sounds make a musical pattern.

Poem is arranged in two four-line stanzas.

Vivid words create a picture of the waves in motion.

All the lines have a similar rhythm.

Each pair of lines rhymes.

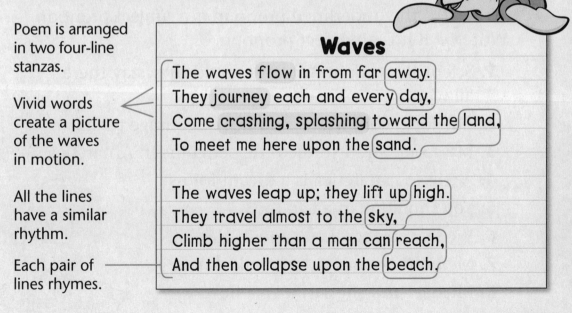

Waves

The waves flow in from far away.
They journey each and every day,
Come crashing, splashing toward the land,
To meet me here upon the sand.

The waves leap up; they lift up high.
They travel almost to the sky,
Climb higher than a man can reach,
And then collapse upon the beach.

Subject and Object Pronouns

A pronoun used as the subject of a sentence is called a **subject pronoun**. A pronoun used after an action verb or as the object of a preposition is called an **object pronoun**.

- *I, you, he, she, it, we,* and *they* are subject pronouns.
- *Me, you, him, her, it, us,* and *them* are object pronouns.

Subject Pronouns   <u>She</u> hiked in the desert.
<u>He</u> and <u>I</u> stayed home.

Object Pronouns   The plants surprised <u>her</u>.
She told <u>him</u> and <u>me</u> about <u>them</u>.

A Write *SP* if the underlined pronoun is a subject pronoun. Write *OP* if it is an object pronoun.

1. Scientists work in Antarctica, and <u>they</u> stay there all winter.

2. The long, cold winters do not discourage <u>them</u>.

3. My group and <u>I</u> studied the penguins in Antarctica.

4. A trip to Antarctica is a dream for <u>us</u>.

5. <u>You</u> should plan a trip too.

6. <u>We</u> saw an active volcano in Hawaii.

7. My brothers and sisters walked near <u>it</u>.

8. Michael and <u>she</u> saw a lava flow.

B Choose the correct pronoun for each sentence. Write the sentence.

1. (We, Us) took a trip to the Grand Canyon.
2. The view of the canyon amazed my cousin and (me, I).
3. Ted and (I, me) photographed the canyon's beautiful colors.
4. Some of (they, them) were red and brown.
5. A guide showed us the canyon, and we talked with (her, she).
6. Dad and (they, them) hiked many trails in the canyon.
7. The river was below (they, them).
8. The depth of the canyon surprised the guide and (him, he).
9. Dad and (he, him) said the deepest point is a mile deep.
10. The hike in the canyon fascinated (we, us).

C Revise each sentence or pair of sentences. Replace the underlined words with subject or object pronouns.

11. The Mississippi River is the longest river in the United States. The Mississippi River is more than 2,000 miles long.
12. Many ships transport cargo on the river. The ships carry millions of tons of freight.
13. Heavy snows and rains fell on the Mississippi River. A flood occurred because of the heavy snows and rains.
14. When Hernando De Soto explored America in 1541, the journey led Hernando De Soto to the Mississippi River.

Test Preparation

 Write the letter of the word that can replace the underlined word or group of words.

1. <u>Those deserts</u> are very hot.

   A They   **C** Him

   B She   **D** Them

2. The desert plants interest <u>Jay</u>.

   A he   **C** him

   B they   **D** us

3. The hot weather agrees with <u>desert animals</u>.

   A it   **C** them

   B they   **D** him

4. Anna and <u>Kate</u> studied snakes.

   A they   **C** she

   B her   **D** them

5. They saw <u>a king snake</u> under the rocks.

   A they   **C** she

   B he   **D** it

6. They showed pictures to Rob and <u>Ted</u>.

   A him   **C** he

   B they   **D** she

7. <u>Rob</u> saw a big toad.

   A Them   **C** He

   B Him   **D** They

8. A jackrabbit hopped by Ty and <u>Kay</u>.

   A she   **C** they

   B her   **D** he

Review

✓ Write *SP* if the underlined pronoun is a subject pronoun. Write *OP* if it is an object pronoun.

1. Ellie went to Japan, and <u>she</u> saw Mount Fuji.
2. It delighted James and <u>her</u>.
3. Ellie's family and <u>he</u> climbed the mountain.
4. She sent a postcard to <u>us</u>.
5. <u>You</u> should see Mount Hood in Oregon.
6. <u>I</u> saw Mount McKinley in Alaska last year.
7. The trip to Alaska was wonderful for Jamal and <u>me</u>.
8. Seeing the highest peak in North America was a thrill for <u>him</u>.

✓ Choose the correct pronoun for each sentence. Write the sentence.

9. (Them, They) climbed Mount Kilimanjaro.
10. Climbing the highest peak in Africa was not hard for (them, they).
11. Jill and (her, she) saw the Matterhorn.
12. This peak in the Alps looked like a pyramid to Jill and (she, her).
13. Raj and (he, him) said the highest peak in California is Mount McKinley.
14. They told (us, we) it is in the Sierra Nevada range.
15. Kelly and (me, I) live in the Rocky Mountains.
16. Pikes Peak is near (we, us).

Style

> **Style** is the quality that makes one piece of writing different from others. There are many features that give each piece of writing a unique style.
>
> - word choice
> - length of sentences
> - kinds of sentences
> - details, including facts, sensory details, and colorful comparisons

Write the word that describes the style of each paragraph.

factual   *imaginative*

1. Once upon a time a family of sky-blue fish set out on a journey. Imagine their surprise when they came upon another fish family. These fish were the coral color of a sunset. Both families traveled on together in bright, shimmery waves. Someday the fish will invite you to visit their ocean. You will see a traveling rainbow!

2. A desert is a place that gets fewer than 10 inches of rain each year. Sand may cover about 10 to 20 percent of a desert. Some of the sand blows into tall dunes. Deserts are dry, but many kinds of plants and animals live there. Plants include cactuses and mesquite trees.

Write a paragraph about your neighborhood. Use a factual or an imaginative style.

Describing a Setting

Setting is the time and place of a story. *Time* is when the story happens, and *place* is where the story happens.

- The description of the setting creates a mood for readers.
- Vivid words help readers see, hear, and smell the place.
- Facts and other details describe the place.

Topic sentence answers where and when about setting.

Vivid verbs create a lively style.

Sensory details describe sights, sounds, and smells of setting.

Saturday Morning in Eastwood

The town of Eastwood sparkles on an early Saturday morning. The sun shines gently on the clean shop windows. The air feels cool and damp. The streets are quiet, and the air smells fresh without the weekday cars and trucks going by. A jogger dashes by, and two dog owners lunge after their pets on early-morning walks. Soon the smells of bacon and coffee float out of the Breadbasket Café. Families will stop by for a hearty breakfast. Then they will head off to soccer games and trips to the zoo. Another busy Saturday has begun!

Possessive Pronouns

Some pronouns show who or what owns, or possesses, something. This kind of pronoun is a **possessive pronoun**. *My, mine, your, yours, her, hers, our, ours, his, their, theirs,* and *its* are possessive pronouns.

• <u>Your</u> rock collection is larger than <u>mine</u>.

A Write the possessive pronoun in each sentence.

1. There are many kinds of rocks in my neighborhood.

2. Your walls and floors are made of rock.

3. The cement in our driveway comes from rocks.

4. Mr. Ferguson used limestone walls in his house.

5. Mrs. Ray used marble floors in hers.

6. Their color is pale gray.

7. That area is beautiful because its rocks are red.

8. Did you see colorful rocks on your hike?

9. I saw yellow and orange rocks on mine.

10. The best views of the mountains are ours.

11. Do you think the best view is yours?

12. The neighbors probably think theirs is the best!

B Choose the possessive pronoun in ( ) that could replace the underlined words in each sentence. Write the sentence.

1. <u>These scientists'</u> work is finding and studying rocks. (Your, Their)

2. Brian's uncle found rocks in <u>Brian's and my</u> neighborhood. (your, our)

3. <u>The scientist's</u> most important find was a black rock. (His, Our)

4. <u>The rock's</u> surface was smooth and shiny. (His, Its)

5. Brian's uncle looked at <u>Brian's</u> rock collection. (his, her)

6. Another scientist looked at <u>the collection I own</u>. (yours, mine)

7. Show the scientist <u>the rocks you own</u>. (hers, yours)

8. The scientists will study <u>the rocks that Brian and I own</u>. (his, ours)

C Revise each sentence. Replace the underlined words with possessive pronouns. Write the sentences.

9. The white cliffs of Dover got that name because <u>the cliffs'</u> limestone is white.

10. Julia and I saw the cliffs with <u>Julia's and my</u> parents.

11. My dad went to England because <u>my dad's</u> company sent him there.

12. When we visited the country, we enjoyed many of <u>the country's</u> sights.

13. Julia's favorite was the Lake District, and <u>my favorite</u> was Stonehenge .

14. Julia took my picture at Stonehenge, and I took <u>Julia's picture</u> in the Lake District.

Test Preparation

✓ Write the letter of the pronoun that correctly completes each sentence.

1. I will show you ____ secret place for finding rocks.

   A my   **C** yours

   B your   **D** its

2. The stones are small, but ____ value is high.

   A our   **C** her

   B their   **D** its

3. These blue rocks are ____ favorites.

   A its   **C** my

   B it's   **D** mine

4. My sister put one on ____ necklace.

   A ours   **C** her

   B theirs   **D** mine

5. The stone is large, and ____ color is bright.

   A their   **C** our

   B her   **D** its

6. I put one in my collection, and you put one in ____.

   A our   **C** my

   B yours   **D** your

7. Ty's green stones are larger than ____.

   A our   **C** my

   B their   **D** mine

8. I found this stone, and I think ____ color is beautiful.

   A it's   **C** its

   B theirs   **D** their

Review

✓ Write the possessive pronoun in each sentence.

1. Chad and Jenny went to a cliff near their house.
2. The cliff had many rocks against its sides.
3. Jenny had a rock hammer in her backpack.
4. Chad said, "My first rock is marble."
5. Chad put seven rocks in his bag.
6. Jenny put nine rocks in hers.
7. All the rocks were theirs.
8. Can you find rocks in your neighborhood?

✓ Choose the possessive pronoun in ( ) that could replace the underlined words in each sentence. Write the sentences.

9. Rocks help us learn how your and my Earth has changed. (our, their)
10. We can see how animals looked from the animals' fossils. (its, their)
11. Mr. Kenny's swamp was home to dinosaurs. (His, Our)
12. A dinosaur was buried in the swamp's mud. (his, its)
13. The dinosaur's bones left the bones' shape in the mud. (its, their)
14. Ms. Shaw's team found many dinosaur fossils. (Her, Hers)
15. Scientists display the scientists' fossils in museums. (their, theirs)
16. I will show you the fossils that I own. (my, mine)

Get Your Reader's Attention

> When you write, **get your reader's attention** from the start. Here are some ways:
>
> - Write a catchy title that puts questions in your reader's mind. To answer the questions, the reader must read your story.
> - Write an opening sentence that creates a vivid image or states an interesting fact.
> - Create suspense. Give clues about the important events. Make your reader curious about what will happen.

Tell how the following sentences get a reader's attention.

1. The sky was as dark as ink, with no moon and no stars. We looked nervously at the sky and then at one another. Would we find what we had come for in this strange place?

Write answers for the following items:

2. Write an opening sentence for a story about an exciting boat trip on rough waters.

3. Write a title for a story about coming face to face with a bear in the woods.

4. You are writing a story about hearing strange sounds while you are camping in your backyard. Write two sentences that will create suspense for your reader.

Memoir

In a **memoir,** a person tells a story about an event in his or her life. The event is often one that changed the writer in some way.

Title makes readers ask, "How *did* the writer become a rock climber?"

First sentence creates a vivid image that makes readers curious.

Facts and images create suspense for readers.

Last two sentences tell how the experience has changed the writer.

How I Became a Rock Climber

I never pictured myself high above the ground, attached to a huge rock. But that's where I was one day last summer. I was visiting my cousins in Colorado, and my uncle drove my cousins and me to a big rock in the desert. It seemed huge! Uncle Dan explained the safety rules to us. He also gave us helmets. What would we need those for?

Uncle Dan put an iron spike into a crack in the rock. He attached a rope to the spike. He showed us how to hold the rope and climb the rock. I was scared at first, and it was hard work. But it was fun! Soon I had climbed higher than I had ever gone in my favorite oak tree. Uncle Dan showed us how to get down. Each week I practice on the rock-climbing equipment at the local gym. I can't wait until next summer's rock-climbing trip in Colorado!

Contractions

A **contraction** is a word made by putting two words together. When words are joined in a contraction, an apostrophe is used to show where a letter or letters have been left out.

- Some contractions combine a pronoun and a verb: *I + will = I'll; they + would = they'd; she + is = she's; it + is = it's; he + has = he's; they + have = they've; you + are = you're.*
- Some contractions combine a verb and *not*: *has + not = hasn't; had + not = hadn't; was + not = wasn't; did + not = didn't; could + not = couldn't; will + not = won't.*

Contractions   We've gone swimming every day, but we won't go tomorrow.

A Write the contraction in each sentence. Then write the words that make up the contraction.

1. Swimming was popular long ago, and it's still popular today.

2. Swimmers began competing in the 1896 Olympics, and they've competed ever since.

3. Women didn't compete in the Olympics until 1912.

4. Wasn't Mark Spitz a winner of seven gold medals in 1972?

5. American swimmers couldn't beat Spitz's record in 2004.

B Write the contraction for the underlined words.

1. My grandpa likes to swim, and <u>he is</u> a good swimmer.
2. He <u>did not</u> swim in a pool when he was young.
3. <u>He would</u> swim in the pond on his parents' farm.
4. He <u>could not</u> wait to dive in on a hot summer day.
5. He <u>had not</u> had swimming lessons.
6. He <u>was not</u> afraid of the frogs and ducks in the pond.
7. <u>They would</u> all swim together.
8. He <u>will not</u> forget his swimming pond.
9. Now <u>he will</u> swim in an indoor pool.
10. Today <u>I will</u> go swimming with Grandpa.

C Expand each group of words to create an interesting sentence. Replace two words in each group of words with a contraction.

11. I am trying out
12. We are practicing
13. My friends are not discouraged
14. We will learn
15. I did not know
16. I had not done
17. It is good to learn
18. The coach says we are
19. The team has not
20. I will be happy

Test Preparation

 Write the letter of the correct contraction for the underlined words.

1. People <u>do not</u> swim just in pools.

   A doesn't   **C** isn't

   B don't   **D** didn't

2. <u>They will</u> swim wherever there is water.

   A They're **C** They'd

   B They'll   **D** Their

3. <u>He is</u> swimming in a lake.

   A He'd   **C** He's

   B She's   **D** His

4. <u>We are</u> in a river.

   A We'd   **C** Were

   B You're   **D** We're

5. I have swum in the ocean when <u>it is</u> warm.

   A it's   **C** I'm

   B its   **D** I'll

6. <u>Have not</u> people swum in the English Channel?

   A Hadnt   **C** Hadn't

   B Hasn't   **D** Haven't

7. You <u>were not</u> swimming in the pond.

   A wasn't   **C** won't

   B weren't **D** we'll

8. Lakes <u>are not</u> as warm as pools.

   A isn't   **C** arent

   B don't   **D** aren't

Review

✓ Write the contraction in each sentence. Then write the words that make up the contraction.

1. She's doing the backstroke in the swim meet.

2. Eddie hasn't done the backstroke before.

3. He'll probably do the butterfly.

4. Maggie didn't practice the breaststroke.

5. She'd like to do the backstroke.

6. Wouldn't you like to practice the butterfly?

7. Tyler won't be at practice tomorrow.

8. He's going to the dentist.

9. I think it's all right to miss practice sometimes.

10. I'm sure Tyler will practice the next day.

✓ Write the contraction for the underlined words.

11. If <u>you are</u> a good swimmer, you can learn to dive.

12. <u>She will</u> dive from a springboard.

13. <u>He has</u> learned to do a forward dive.

14. She <u>is not</u> ready to do a half-twist.

15. His body <u>was not</u> straight when he hit the water.

16. <u>They will</u> practice before the meet.

17. <u>She is</u> jumping at the end of the board.

18. She <u>does not</u> jump high enough.

19. <u>They are</u> applauding for her.

20. They <u>could not</u> believe how good she was.

Supporting Details

> **Supporting details** in your writing should give more information about the main idea. For example, if you want to describe the way something looks or feels, your supporting details should be vivid descriptions. If your purpose is to inform your reader, your supporting details should be facts.

 Write the sentence from each paragraph that is not a supporting detail.

1. Members of our community swim team work hard. Swimming is fun for the members. Team members must train five days each week. They must swim for one hour each day.

2. I had always wanted to participate in the diving competition. I stood high atop the diving board, feeling strong and confident. Then I decided that I did not want to dive. I knew I could perform one of my best dives ever in front of dozens of people.

 Write one supporting detail for each main idea.

3. My first swimming lesson was an interesting experience.

4. Everyone should learn to swim at a young age.

5. Swimming is an excellent form of exercise.

Describing a Goal

When **describing a goal,** a writer tells about something that he or she wanted to achieve and did achieve. The writer uses supporting details that tell how the goal was reached and why it was meaningful.

My 5K Race

First paragraph gives background information.

Each year our school has a field day. Students compete in running and jumping events. I didn't compete last year. There was only one event I wanted to enter: the 5-kilometer race. A 5K is not a quick sprint like the 50-yard dash. Running five kilometers takes endurance. I decided to enter next year's 5K race.

Details explain how the writer prepared to reach the goal.

My brother helped me train three days a week at the school track. At first I ran out of breath quickly. My side hurt. Soon I could run three kilometers without stopping. I was slow at first, but each week I felt stronger. Sometimes I felt as if I could run forever! When field day rolled around, I was ready.

Details describe how the goal was finally reached.

Halfway through, two other runners and I led the race. The stiff competition made me even stronger. I won the race!

Last three sentences tell why accomplishing the goal was meaningful.

I was thrilled, but not because I beat other runners. I had set a tough goal. I had achieved it through hard work.

Prepositions

A **preposition** is the first word in a group of words called a prepositional phrase. A **prepositional phrase** ends with a noun or pronoun called the **object of the preposition**. A prepositional phrase tells more about other words in a sentence.

Preposition	The eagle lived <u>on</u> a cliff.
Prepositional Phrase	The eagle lived <u>on a cliff</u>.
Object of Preposition	The eagle lived on a <u>cliff</u>.

Here are some prepositions: *about, above, across, after, against, along, among, around, at, before, behind, below, beneath, beside, between, beyond, by, down, during, except, for, from, in, inside, into, near, of, off, on, onto, out, outside, over, past, since, through, throughout, to, toward, under, underneath, until, up, upon, with, within, without.*

A Write the preposition in each sentence.

1. My family drove through the Rocky Mountains.
2. A huge bird flew across the sky.
3. It settled above a rocky cliff.
4. It stopped beside a huge nest.
5. Inside the nest, baby eagles rested.
6. The word for a baby eagle is *eaglet*.
7. An eaglet is covered with fuzz.
8. Eaglets leave the nest after 12 weeks.

B Write the prepositional phrase in each sentence. Underline the preposition.

   1. Are eagles the strongest birds in the world?

   2. They fly even during bad weather.

   3. Eagles stay far from people.

   4. The golden eagle has been called the "king of birds."

   5. An eagle has strong claws on its feet.

   6. It carries prey with its claws.

   7. Eagles are among the heaviest birds.

   8. They glide high above the trees.

   9. An eagle catches a fish near the water's edge.

10. It uses its wings for paddles.

11. The eagle carries its prey to its nest.

12. It tears the fish into pieces.

C Choose a preposition from the box that makes sense in each sentence. Write the sentences.

inside	upon	without	across	of	to

13. A nest ____ eagles is called an aerie.

14. Each year, the eagle returns ____ the same aerie.

15. Eagles lay eggs ____ their aeries.

16. The mother eagle sits ____ the eggs.

17. The father eagle flies ____ the valley.

18. He does not return ____ food.

Test Preparation

 Write the letter of the word in each sentence that is a preposition.

1. An eagle flies over the lake.

  A An   **C** the

  B over   **D** lake

2. It dives into the water.

  A It   **C** into

  B dives   **D** water

3. A bald eagle sits upon a branch.

  A bald   **C** a

  B branch   **D** upon

4. White feathers grow on its head.

  A head   **C** on

  B its   **D** grow

5. In the wilderness there are many eagles.

  A In   **C** there

  B the   **D** are

6. A nest near the water holds two eggs.

  A nest   **C** the

  B near   **D** holds

7. A baby eagle with white fuzz hatches.

  A with   **C** fuzz

  B white   **D** hatches

8. A big eagle brings food to the nest.

  A big   **C** to

  B food   **D** nest

Review

✓ Write the preposition in each sentence.

1. Golden eagles live throughout North America.
2. They have golden brown feathers on their necks.
3. The harpy eagle lives within the rain forest.
4. It is known for its yellow feet.
5. The serpent eagle of Asia eats snakes.
6. The rain forest is home to the Philippine eagle.
7. Steppe eagles fly over Egypt each year.
8. A harsh call is made by the African fish eagle.
9. About 40 years ago, bald eagles were endangered.
10. Their numbers have increased since that time.

✓ Write the prepositional phrase in each sentence. Underline the preposition.

11. My cousin from Arizona is a birdwatcher.
12. He finds many birds outside his house.
13. He views them through strong lenses.
14. He saw a huge golden eagle in the desert.
15. A woodpecker with a red head perched nearby.
16. A little roadrunner jogged past him.
17. An owl sat upon a cactus.
18. Sparrows and wrens fly around him.
19. A quail hurries along the ground.
20. My cousin looks at birds until dark.

Transitions to Show Order

Events in a story happen in a certain order.
Transition words and phrases such as *first,
then, later,* and *after a while* show the order of
the events.

 Write the word or phrase that shows order.

> **1.** Jacob saw a bird's nest. Later, he looked at the nest
> through his binoculars.
>
> **2.** After a while, Jacob saw a big hawk swoop into the tree.

 Add a phrase from the box or your
own word or phrase to each sentence.

during the day	on Saturday
at night	on Sunday

> **3.** Molly went birdwatching in the woods. She went
> birdwatching at the pond.
>
> **4.** The owl slept on the tree stump. The owl hunted
> for food.

 Write two or three sentences
about something that happened
in your backyard, a park, or
another natural place. Use
transitions to show the order
of events.

Writing for Tests

Prompt   Describe the <u>plot</u>, or <u>important events,</u> of a <u>story</u>. Tell what happens in the story to a <u>friend who has not read it.</u>

Plot summary begins with first story event. Other events are described in time order.

Words and phrases show when each event happens.

Summary tells main events of the plot but not all the details.

Goldilocks and the Three Bears

A little girl, Goldilocks, goes inside a house in the woods. In the kitchen, she sits in each chair. One is too big and one is too little, but the third one is the right size. Next Goldilocks tests the porridge on the table. One bowl is too hot and one is too cold, but the third is just right. By now Goldilocks is tired, so she goes upstairs to the bedroom. One bed is too hard and one is too soft. The third one is just right, and Goldilocks falls asleep. Meanwhile, the mother, father, and baby bear who live in the house return home. They see that someone has used their chairs and eaten their food. They go upstairs and find Goldilocks. Goldilocks awakens to see the bears looking at her. Frightened, she runs away and never wanders into the woods again.

Adjectives and Articles

An **adjective** is a word that can describe a person, place, or thing. Adjectives tell more about nouns. A, *an,* and *the* are special adjectives called **articles.**

Adjectives <u>Many</u> people wore <u>bright</u> clothes to the <u>annual</u> parade.

Articles <u>The</u> child wore <u>an</u> orange sweater and <u>a</u> blue jacket.

- The articles *a* and *an* are used only with singular nouns. *A* is used before a word that begins with a consonant sound: *a box, a red coat. An* is used before a word that begins with a vowel sound: *an egg, an empty box, an old coat.*

- Use *the* before singular or plural nouns: *the earring, the earrings.*

A Write the adjective that describes each underlined noun.

1. A kimono is made of vivid <u>cloth</u>.

2. The Japanese wear kimonos for special <u>occasions</u>.

3. They wear wide <u>belts</u> with their kimonos.

4. We will wear fancy <u>kimonos</u> to the party.

Write the article in ( ) that correctly completes each sentence.

5. In Hawaii, a muumuu is (a, an) long dress.

6. I bought (a, an) attractive muumuu in Honolulu.

7. My dad bought (an, the) brightest shirt he could find.

B Write the adjectives, including the articles, in each sentence. The number in ( ) tells you how many are in the sentence.

1. Noriko took a long trip to faraway Japan. (3)
2. She stayed with elderly Aunt Chiyoko. (1)
3. She loved the bright, noisy city of Tokyo. (3)
4. Aunt Chiyoko had a small apartment. (2)
5. The family ate dinner at a low table. (3)
6. They ate some unusual fish with delicious sauce. (3)
7. Noriko and Aunt Chiyoko visited an elegant garden. (2)
8. The small, fancy trees in the garden were called *bonsai*. (4)
9. One was an evergreen bonsai. (2)
10. Noriko had an excellent time on the trip. (3)

C Add an adjective for each blank. Write the new sentences.

11. The ___ garden had ___ flowers.
12. A ___ tree was covered with ___ blossoms.
13. The ___ weather signaled an ___ spring.
14. ___ people walked among the ___ beds of flowers.
15. Two ___ rabbits hopped around a ___ bush.

Test Preparation

 Write the letter of the word that is an adjective.

1. The team is playing a big game.

   A team   **C** big

   B playing   **D** game

2. The players are wearing orange shirts.

   A players   **C** shirts

   B are   **D** orange

3. Most of them have sturdy shoes.

   A Most   **C** shoes

   B sturdy   **D** them

4. The other players have green shirts.

   A other   **C** have

   B players   **D** shirts

5. Each one wears long socks.

   A one   **C** long

   B wears   **D** socks

6. Some girls are dancing after school.

   A after   **C** girls

   B school   **D** Some

7. The dancers wear soft shoes.

   A soft   **C** dancers

   B shoes   **D** wear

8. They attend class in the new gym.

   A new   **C** attend

   B gym   **D** class

Review

☑ Write the adjective that describes each underlined noun.

1. Many <u>holidays</u> are celebrated in Japan.

2. Popular <u>celebrations</u> include the New Year's Day Festival.

3. People wear fancy <u>kimonos</u>.

4. Many tie red <u>belts</u> around their kimonos.

5. Wide <u>sashes</u> are called *obis*.

6. Cities and towns have colorful <u>parades</u>.

7. Families have splendid <u>feasts</u>.

8. People give nice <u>gifts</u> to their friends and family.

9. Some <u>people</u> celebrate for several days.

10. Special <u>festivities</u> such as these are fun for everyone.

☑ Choose the article in ( ) that correctly completes each sentence. Write the sentence.

11. Midori is writing (a, an) unusual kind of poem.

12. (An, The) poem is from Japan and is called a *haiku*.

13. It is (a, an) very short poem.

14. It describes (a, an) interesting part of nature.

15. Japan has (a, an) fascinating kind of theater too.

16. (A, The) actors often portray characters from history.

17. (A, The) makeup on these players is unusual.

18. (A, The) players are all men.

Strong Adjectives

> **Strong adjectives** describe nouns in a specific, lively way. Strong adjectives help readers see, hear, feel, taste, and touch what the writer is describing.

 Find four strong adjectives in each set of sentences. Write the adjectives.

1. The dancers wore baggy pants with brilliant shirts and soft velvet vests.

2. The music made a jolly clattering as the energetic performers bounced across the glossy wooden floor of the ballroom.

3. The enthusiastic singer let out a shrill note that could be heard by the noisy dancers all the way across the enormous ballroom.

Add a strong adjective to describe each underlined noun. Write the sentences. Underline the adjectives.

4. The <u>crowd</u> cheered as the <u>players</u> ran onto the <u>field</u>.

5. Several <u>police officers</u> stopped the <u>bystanders</u> outside the <u>gates</u>.

6. The <u>children</u> rushed into the <u>hall</u> as their <u>father</u> came in the door.

Editorial

> An **editorial** appears in a newspaper or magazine.
> An editorial states the writer's opinion about a topic.
> It supports the opinion with facts and examples.

First sentence states the writer's opinion.

Writer uses strong adjectives to make the details lively and persuasive.

Second paragraph contains facts and examples that support the writer's opinion.

All Students Should Wear School Uniforms

I think students in public schools should wear uniforms. I visited two schools last week. At one school, all the students wore neat blue pants and clean white shirts. At the other school, the students wore a jumble of styles, from torn jeans to expensive leather jackets. The students with uniforms were polite. Students at the school without uniforms seemed disorganized and rude.

First of all, uniforms make students' lives easier. With uniforms, kids don't have to think about what to wear each day, and they don't need to worry about being in style. Second, uniforms make students feel they are part of a group. This makes them work hard together. Their neat appearance makes them behave more politely.

Students can express their personalities with their clothes on weekends. But during the school day, uniforms are the way to go!

Adjectives That Compare

Adjectives are often used to make comparisons. To compare two people, places, or things, you usually add -er to an adjective. To compare three or more people, places, or things, you usually add -est to an adjective.

Puerto Rico has <u>warmer</u> weather than Florida.

Northern Africa has the <u>warmest</u> weather of all.

Sometimes you must change the spelling of an adjective when you write the -er or -est form.

Drop final e	rare rarer rarest
Change y to i	spicy spicier spiciest
Double final consonant	hot hotter hottest

A Write the adjective that compares in each sentence.

1. My family had a longer stay in China than in Kenya.
2. I think China has the strangest animals in the world.
3. The giant panda is the heaviest panda of all.
4. Pandas have the oddest diets of any animal.
5. To them, bamboo plants are tastier than fruits.
6. Of the two countries, my family had a nicer time in Kenya.
7. We saw the brightest cloth in the world at the market.
8. We had the hottest day I can remember.
9. The night was cooler than the day.
10. The air is thinner in the mountains than along the coast.

B Choose the adjective in ( ) that correctly completes each sentence. Write the sentences.

1. Which is the (greater, greatest) sport of all?
2. Soccer attracts the (bigger, biggest) crowds in the world.
3. Baseball has (larger, largest) crowds here than in Mexico.
4. Are baseball players (stronger, strongest) than golfers?
5. Cricket is the (stranger, strangest) game I have ever seen.
6. It is usually a (longer, longest) game than baseball.
7. Are baseball rules (clearer, clearest) than cricket rules?
8. Football has the (louder, loudest) fans of any sport.
9. Basketball is the (easier, easiest) sport of all.
10. Is basketball the (cooler, coolest) sport in the world?

C Complete each sentence by adding the *-er* or *-est* form of an adjective in the box. Use each adjective only once. Write the new sentences.

pretty	cheap	busy	nice	rich

11. That city has the ___ market in the world.
12. The pottery is ___ than the pottery at home.
13. Some shoppers are ___ than others.
14. The daisies are the ___flowers I have ever seen.
15. The vegetables are ___ than those in the grocery store.

Test Preparation

 Write the letter of the word that correctly completes each sentence.

1. Juan's new house is ___ than his old house.

   A biger
   B bigger
   C biggest
   D more bigger

2. His yard is the ___ one he has ever seen.

   A larger
   B largeer
   C largest
   D largeest

3. His school is the ___ school in the city.

   A old
   B oldest
   C older
   D most older

4. He lives in a ___ neighborhood than before.

   A quieter
   B quiet
   C more quietest
   D quietest

5. Anna's new house is ___ than her old house.

   A fancy
   B fanciest
   C fancyest
   D fancier

6. Her bedroom is the ___ room in the house.

   A tinyer
   B tiniest
   C tinyest
   D tiny

Review

☑ Write the adjective that compares in each sentence.

1. Grandpa is the greatest storyteller in the world.
2. He is also the thinnest family member from Puerto Rico.
3. He says Puerto Rico is the loveliest country of all.
4. It has the finest people in the world.
5. His tales of Puerto Rico are funnier than Uncle Luis's.
6. His jokes are even sillier than mine.
7. Sometimes Grandpa acts even stranger than I do.
8. He is the cleverest member of our family.
9. I can't think of a family jollier than ours.
10. We have the happiest times of all with Grandpa.

☑ Choose the adjective in ( ) that correctly completes each sentence. Write the sentences.

11. Who can make the (tastier, tastiest) pizza, Ed or you?
12. I will use the (spicier, spiciest) sauce in the kitchen.
13. Then I will add the (hotter, hottest) sausage I can find.
14. These mushrooms are (fresher, freshest) than those.
15. This cheese is (mild, milder) than the other kind.
16. Those tomatoes are (sweeter, sweetest) than usual.
17. The peppers are the (green, greenest) ones I have ever seen.
18. The oven is (warmer, warmest) than before.
19. I am a (finer, finest) cook than Ed.
20. My pizza is the (rich, richest) pizza ever!

Persuasive Words

Persuasive words are words that state a judgment made by the writer. Some persuasive words are *should, must, best, worst, most,* and adjectives ending in *-est.* They are used to get readers to agree with the writer's opinion.

   You <u>should</u> try a Chinese meal <u>because</u> it includes the <u>healthiest</u> and <u>tastiest</u> foods in the world. It has the <u>most interesting</u> variety of foods.

 Find three persuasive words or phrases in each set of sentences. Write the persuasive words and phrases.

   1. You should visit Africa. The friendliest people live there, and they have the most unusual stories to tell.

   2. That part of the park is the worst place to camp of all. It has the ugliest scenery and the coldest water.

   3. Everyone must get together to clean up our downtown. We have the nicest neighborhoods and best schools in the county, so why is our downtown area so dirty?

Write details to support the following opinion. Use at least three persuasive words or phrases in your details.

You should root for my favorite team.

Writing Your Opinion

In **writing your opinion,** you state a strong viewpoint about a topic. Your purpose is to persuade your readers to agree with you. Support your opinion with facts, examples, and descriptions.

Writer asks questions to attract readers' attention.

Sentence states writer's opinion.

Facts and descriptions support writer's opinion.

Writer uses persuasive words.

The Best Place to Live

Would you like to live in a place that is warm all year? Would you like a place where flowers brighten all four seasons? Would you like a place where the nicest people in the world live? Then you would love Florida! I think Florida is the best place to live.

Florida has the most beautiful scenery in the world. Relax and observe the wading birds and mangrove trees in the Everglades. Lie on a white sandy beach and feel the gentle breeze blow through the palm trees. Do you like amusement parks and sea parks? You will find the most fun parks in Florida. Florida has big, busy cities such as Miami and quiet wilderness areas as well. Here's the best thing about Florida: my family lives here! Florida is the greatest place to live in the world.

Adverbs

An **adverb** is a word that can tell when, where, or how something happens.

<u>Yesterday</u>, the family moved into a new home. (when)

They carried boxes <u>inside</u>. (where)

They <u>happily</u> unpacked the boxes. (how)

- Adverbs can come before or after the verbs they describe.
- Adverbs that tell how something happens often end in *-ly.*

A Write the adverb in each sentence.

1. Recently Jangmi said good-bye to her house in Korea.
2. Then she left the house.
3. She wandered around.
4. Jangmi quietly looked at her big bedroom.
5. She now was happy about her new home.
6. The house has a playroom downstairs.
7. There is a beautiful garden outside.
8. The builders arranged the bricks beautifully on the new house.
9. The painters carefully painted each room.
10. The workers cleaned the house thoroughly.
11. Jangmi will unpack her boxes later.
12. Finally, the house will belong to its new owners.

B Write the adverb in each sentence. Then write whether the adverb tells *when, where,* or *how.*

1. The Wilsons often discuss their need for a new home.
2. Today Maria suggested a familiar city neighborhood.
3. Maria's dad had a store there.
4. Dad supported Maria's suggestion heartily.
5. Tom always had wanted an oceanside home.
6. Then Maria's mom mentioned a pretty little town.
7. Both the city and the beach were nearby.
8. Surprisingly, everyone liked Mom's idea.
9. The family quickly made their plans.
10. Soon they will find a new home in the town.

C Make each sentence more specific by adding an adverb from the box. Write the new sentences. Use each adverb only once.

often	fondly	soon	eagerly	first	later

11. Will's family looks forward to their trip to Korea.
12. They will go to the capital city of Seoul.
13. They will go to a village near the sea.
14. Will's parents have described their native country.
15. They remember their early years in Korea.
16. The whole family will have memories of Korea.

Test Preparation

 Write the letter of the word that is an adverb.

1. Today the class is studying Korea.

   A is   **C** class

   B studying **D** Today

2. Lee hardly remembers his years in Korea.

   A remembers **C** hardly

   B his   **D** years

3. The country has grown rapidly.

   A rapidly **C** has

   B grown   **D** country

4. People are everywhere on the streets.

   A are   **C** People

   B everywhere **D** on

5. Korea usually has had close ties to Japan.

   A has   **C** close

   B usually **D** ties

6. The people generally speak Korean.

   A people **C** speak

   B generally **D** Korean

7. Families have always respected older people.

   A people **C** always

   B older   **D** have

8. Sometimes people wear traditional clothes.

   A wear   **C** clothes

   B traditional **D** Sometimes

9. People in Korea eat rice often.

   A often   **C** in

   B People **D** rice

10. Pictures clearly show Korea's charm.

   A show   **C** clearly

   B Pictures **D** show

Review

☑ Write the adverb in each sentence.

1. Yesterday I studied holidays in other countries.

2. Koreans celebrate the fall harvest annually.

3. The holiday is interestingly called the Moon Festival.

4. In China, people happily celebrate the Chinese New Year.

5. They have colorful parades outside.

6. The French joyfully celebrate independence on Bastille Day.

7. It always occurs on July 14.

8. May Day is celebrated differently in different places.

9. People often celebrate springtime on May Day.

10. Many countries honor their workers then.

☑ Write the adverb in each sentence. Then write whether the adverb tells *when, where,* or *how.*

11. Homes everywhere have different characteristics.

12. Japanese homes usually have straw mats on floors.

13. Korean floors have heat pipes underneath.

14. Some Africans firmly pack mud for walls.

15. In parts of Mongolia, people may set up tents anyplace.

16. American builders work differently in each area.

17. New Orleans designers often decorate homes with wrought iron.

18. Builders frequently make East Coast homes from brick.

Use Reasons to Persuade

When your goal is to convince readers to buy a product or use a service, **use reasons to persuade** them. A reason is a specific answer to the question "Why?" When you want readers to take an action, give them logical, specific reasons why they should act. Use vivid descriptive words and persuasive words in your reasons.

You should visit Hawaii. It has the <u>most beautiful beaches</u>. It has the <u>warmest, sunniest weather all year</u>.

Read the ad. Then write answers to the questions.

Visit San Antonio, Texas. You can stroll along the River Walk and enjoy a meal outdoors. Go to the Alamo and see where history was made. Attend the colorful Fiesta San Antonio in April or go to the annual rodeo in February.

1. What does the writer want to persuade readers to do?

2. What reasons does the writer use to persuade readers?

Write two reasons to persuade readers to take each action.

3. Come to the school fair.

4. Join the soccer team.

Ad

> **Ads** are written to convince readers to buy a product or use a service. Ads use persuasive words, reasons, and vivid descriptions to encourage readers to act.

Writer begins to list reasons why people should visit Washington.

Writer uses vivid descriptions to appeal to readers' senses.

Writer includes persuasive words to convince readers.

Come to Washington, D.C.

Are you looking for the perfect family vacation? Then visit Washington, D.C.! Washington has many exciting museums, such as the National Air and Space Museum. The Jefferson Memorial and other beautiful monuments sit elegantly on the green banks of the Potomac River. In spring white blossoms bloom on the cherry trees along the river. Of course, the best reason to visit Washington is to see where American history was made. You can visit the Capitol and see our government at work. You can also visit the White House and see where Abraham Lincoln lived. You could spend two weeks in Washington, D.C., and still not see all the educational and inspiring sights. Make your plans today to come to our nation's capital.

Adverbs That Compare

You can use **adverbs** to compare actions. The *-er* form of an adverb compares two actions. The *-est* form of an adverb compares three or more actions.

That baker's cakes rise <u>high</u>.
That baker's cakes rise <u>higher</u> than Mr. Lee's cakes.
That baker's cakes rise <u>highest</u> of any cakes.

Most adverbs that end in *-ly* use *more* and *most* to make comparisons.

Tom ate breakfast <u>slowly</u>.
Tom ate breakfast <u>more slowly</u> than Alison.
Tom ate breakfast <u>most slowly</u> of all the children.

A Write the adverb that compares in each sentence.

1. Mrs. Sanchez works harder than the bakery's owner.

2. Mr. Lane rolls out pastry dough more rapidly than Ms. Delroy.

3. Mrs. Sanchez makes delicious treats fastest of all the bakers.

4. The sweet rolls disappear most quickly of all.

5. One oven cooks faster than the other oven.

6. Everyone worked more carefully than usual.

7. Mrs. Sanchez was finished sooner than the others.

8. Her scones baked most rapidly of all.

9. Mrs. Fisher's bagels took longer than Ms. Delroy's turnovers.

10. Mr. Ling's muffins cooked slowest of all.

B Choose the correct word in ( ) to complete each sentence. Write the sentences.

1. Of all her family members, Sharon cooked (more often, most often).

2. She chose a career (earlier, earliest) than her friend Dave did.

3. She decided (sooner, soonest) than Dave to be a chef.

4. Of all the students in her cooking class, Sharon studied (harder, hardest).

5. She prepared food (more quickly, most quickly) than her best friend.

6. She kneaded bread (more rapidly, most rapidly) of all the bakers in class.

7. Sharon cooked in her restaurant (more confidently, most confidently) than her assistant.

8. She baked (more creatively, most creatively) of any chef in the city.

9. She chose vegetables (more carefully, most carefully) than her chief rival.

C Complete each sentence. Use the *-er* or *-est* form of an adverb in the box. Use each adverb only once.

fast	calmly	often

10. Pablo makes tacos ____ than Manuel.

11. Tom cooks spaghetti ____ than Paul does.

12. Of all his friends, Taylor works ____ in the kitchen.

Test Preparation

✓ Write the letter of the word that correctly completes each sentence.

1. Stacy tries new foods ____ than Tim.

    A often

    B more often

    C most often

    D oftenest

2. Tim eats sandwiches ____ than salads.

    A eagerly

    B most eagerly

    C eagerer

    D more eagerly

3. Stacy eats vegetables ____ than meats.

    A frequently

    B frequenter

    C more frequently

    D most frequently

4. Of all her neighbors, Stacy grows vegetables ____.

    A easy

    B more easily

    C more easy

    D most easily

5. She plants tomatoes ____ than carrots.

    A earlier

    B earliest

    C early

    D most earliest

6. She waits for them to ripen ____ than I do.

    A patiently

    B most patiently

    C more patiently

    D patienter

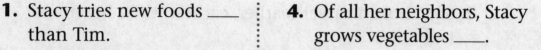

Review

✓ Write the adverb that compares in each sentence.

   1. Of all her sisters, Charla awakens earliest.

   2. She waits for breakfast more eagerly than Michelle.

   3. The bagels toast longer than usual.

   4. Michelle waits more patiently than Charla does.

   5. Tamara pours cereal more carefully this morning than yesterday.

   6. Charla eats breakfast fastest of anyone in the family.

   7. Tamara eats breakfast more calmly than her sister.

   8. Of the three girls, Michelle goes to school most enthusiastically.

✓ Choose the correct word in ( ) to complete each sentence. Write the sentences.

   9. Of all the people in the neighborhood, Mr. Green cooks (more skillfully, most skillfully).

   10. He makes pie crust (more rapidly, most rapidly) than the French chef does.

   11. Of all his friends, he makes tacos (faster, fastest).

   12. He puts a pizza together (more quickly, most quickly) than Dana does.

   13. He tries new recipes (most fearlessly, more fearlessly) than Edward does.

   14. Mr. Green prepares a feast (most calmly, more calmly) of all the cooks I know.

WRITER'S CRAFT

Put Reasons in Order

When you use reasons to persuade readers or to explain your opinion, **put the reasons in order**. You might begin with your least important reason and end with your most important reason. You can signal your most important reason with a phrase such as *best of all* or *most important*.

 Read the first sentence of each paragraph and the reasons that support it. Then write the letters of the sentences to show the best order for a good paragraph.

1. You should eat green vegetables as often as possible.

A Most importantly, green vegetables have many vitamins that will make you healthy.

B First of all, green vegetables look bright and colorful on the dinner table.

C In addition, there are many delicious recipes for green vegetables.

2. Try baking your own breads and rolls at home.

A Baking bread fills your home with wonderful aromas.

B Best of all, baked goods are delicious treats for your family and friends.

C Better yet, baking is fun and creative.

Why is it important to eat a good breakfast? Write three or four sentences to answer this question. Put your reasons in order. Signal your most important reason with a phrase.

Answer a Question

> When you are writing to **answer a question**, give reasons to explain your answer. Put your reasons in order, from least important to most important.

First sentence states writer's opinion.

Remaining sentences give reasons for writer's opinion. They are arranged in order from least important to most important.

Reasons include vivid sensory details to get readers' attention.

What is your favorite food?

My favorite food is spaghetti. I like spaghetti because it is Italian like my grandma. In fact, my grandma makes the best spaghetti in the world. Spaghetti is great for a quick lunch or a nice family dinner. It's the perfect meal when I'm hungry. You can easily prepare other foods to serve with spaghetti, such as a crisp green salad and hot garlic bread. Spaghetti has many nourishing things in it. Pasta has protein plus carbohydrates for energy. The tomato sauce has meat in it, which also contains protein. The tomatoes are full of Vitamin C. Most importantly, I like spaghetti because it tastes delicious!

Conjunctions

A **conjunction** is a word that connects words or groups of words.

• To add information, use the conjunction *and*. To show a difference, use the conjunction *but*. To show a choice, use the conjunction *or*.

James played ball <u>and</u> listened to music.

He had never played stickball, <u>but</u> he enjoyed it.

He could stay inside <u>or</u> play outside.

• You can use a conjunction to combine two sentences into a compound sentence. Add a comma before the conjunction in a compound sentence.

James had played baseball. He had never played stickball.

James had played baseball, but he had never played stickball.

A Write the conjunction in each sentence.

1. New York is a huge city, but it has many smaller neighborhoods.

2. Many artists and writers live in Greenwich Village.

3. Central Park has gardens, playgrounds, and a zoo.

4. You can see a play or a musical near Times Square.

5. Harlem is in New York City, and it is an interesting neighborhood.

B Choose the correct word in ( ) to complete each sentence. Write the sentences.

1. You can view art at museums (but, and) galleries.

2. You can go for the day (but, or) for an hour.

3. The museum has some very old art, (or, but) it has new pieces too.

4. You can take a tour (or, but) wander around alone.

5. You can't see everything in one day, (and, but) you can always come back.

6. One gallery has sculptures, (and, or) another has collages.

7. You can just view the art, (and, or) you can buy it.

8. Often you can meet an artist (but, or) hear the artist speak.

9. That gallery is small, (but, or) it has some wonderful paintings.

10. Art galleries are fun, (or, and) they are educational as well.

C Combine each pair of sentences using *and, but,* or *or.* Write the new sentences. Remember that compound sentences need commas.

11. The painting shows Boston. The collage shows New York.

12. The styles are different. Both pieces of art show the liveliness of cities.

13. The picture was painted in 2001. It shows a scene from the 1800s.

14. See the collage in person. View it on the Internet.

15. Some artists painted Boston. Many more painted New York.

Test Preparation

 Write the letter of the word that best completes each sentence.

1. Dan likes sightseeing, ____ Jo likes it too.

  A unless **C** and
  B only   **D** or

2. Dan likes museums, ____ he likes parks better.

  A or   **C** and
  B but   **D** since

3. Jo likes the science museum, ____ Dan prefers the art museum.

  A but   **C** since
  B or   **D** with

4. Jo likes tall buildings ____ big stores.

  A but   **C** since
  B and   **D** while

5. Dan would prefer a zoo ____ a playground.

  A but   **C** yet
  B nor   **D** or

6. The city has all of these ____ more.

  A and   **C** since
  B or   **D** nor

7. Sightseeing is fun, ____ it is tiring.

  A and   **C** since
  B but   **D** with

8. At the end of the day, you can stop ____ rest.

  A but   **C** and
  B yet   **D** because

Review

✓ Write the conjunction in each sentence.

1. We went to the Empire State Building and rode to the top.

2. It has 102 stories and is 1,250 feet high.

3. It was once the world's tallest building, but it is not anymore.

4. You can see the city from the 86th or the 102nd floor.

5. The Empire State Building is a famous sight, but it is also a busy office building.

6. There are pictures at the library or on the Internet.

7. You should go to New York City and see this building.

8. You cannot see a building this tall in Texas or in Florida.

✓ Write the correct word in ( ) to complete each sentence.

9. The parks in my town are nice, (or, but) they are not like Central Park.

10. Central Park is in New York City, (but, and) it is 2½ miles long.

11. You can visit the park's zoo (but, or) bird house.

12. Outside the park is noisy traffic, (and, but) inside is peace and quiet.

13. You can take a picnic (or, but) get a snack in the park.

14. People walk, skate, (but, and) jog in the park.

Know Your Audience

> When your goal is to persuade readers to agree with your viewpoint, you need to **know your audience.** To know your audience, think about the age, interests, and opinions of your readers. Keep these in mind as you choose your details.

Tell for which audience each paragraph was written.

third graders	nature lovers	high-school students

1. *Winter Dreams* by F. Scott Fitzgerald tells the story of a young man who wants to marry a young woman from a wealthy family. The story takes place in the 1920s, but anyone who worries about going to college, getting a job, and someday getting married will enjoy it.

2. Whales face many dangers, such as icebergs and polluted waters. Everyone wants to protect whales and other sea animals. *A Symphony of Whales* is an inspiring story about a girl who comes up with a unique way to help a group of whales stuck in an icy sea.

3. *Suki's Kimono* is a great story about a young girl who wears what she wants no matter what her classmates think. If you've ever worn something that others didn't think was cool, or even if you've wanted to, you'll love this story.

Story Review

> In a **story review,** you explain to readers why they should read a particular story or not. You describe what you like and dislike about the story.

First two sentences state writer's opinions of story. ──

Writer supports opinion with reasons. Transitions show order of reasons. ──

Writer ends with most important reason and tells readers what they should do. ──

A True-to-Life Story

Me and Uncle Romie is a story that will make you both happy and sad. You will enjoy reading about the main character, James. First of all, the story has a colorful setting. James goes to New York City for the first time. It is fun to read about the city's sights and James's responses to them. Second, the story's characters seem real. James is happy sometimes. Other times he is unsure of himself, sad, or homesick. Everyone can identify with these feelings. Finally, James has interesting relationships with his aunt and uncle. At the story's beginning, he does not know these family members. By the end, he knows both them and himself much better. This story will remind readers of their own unique family members. For an enjoyable reading experience, read *Me and Uncle Romie*.

Capital Letters

Use **capital letters** for proper nouns. Proper nouns include days of the week, months of the year, and holidays. Titles for people and abbreviations of the titles should be capitalized when they are used with a person's name. Do not capitalize titles when they are used by themselves.

Incorrect	The fourth thursday in november is thanksgiving.
Correct	The fourth Thursday in November is Thanksgiving.
Incorrect	My Grandpa visits on hanukkah and labor day.
Correct	My grandpa visits on Hanukkah and Labor Day.

A Write correctly the words in each sentence that should have capital letters. If a sentence has no capitalization mistakes, write *C*.

1. Today dr. chang said Americans have many symbols of freedom.

2. My mom and dad display our flag each july.

3. That is when our country celebrates independence day.

4. Some people display flags from january to december.

5. One monday in june I spotted a bald eagle.

6. Bald eagles stand for freedom in the United States.

B Write the sentences. Use capital letters correctly.

1. The art students are taking a trip with ms. collins in february.

2. They will see a statue of mr. lincoln on presidents' day.

3. On tuesday they will visit a statue of president Washington.

4. They will also see wooden carvings in mr. toma's studio.

5. They will see bronze statues on wednesday.

6. On thursday, february 25, the students plan to study paintings of cowboys.

7. Stacy's uncle will show us his marble statues on friday.

8. He made aunt Ellen a statue for valentine's day.

9. On saturday, everyone will return to New York.

10. Next year the art trip will take place over memorial day.

C Answer each question with a complete sentence. Use capital letters correctly.

11. Which holiday did you celebrate most recently?

12. In what month does this holiday occur?

13. What is a holiday for which you receive gifts?

14 On which day of the week do you get up latest?

15. In which month did you go on a trip away from home?

16. Who is your favorite coach?

Test Preparation

 Write the letter of the word or words that should be capitalized. If no words should be capitalized, choose *none*.

1. My family saw the Statue of Liberty in july.

   A none

   B saw

   C july

   D family

2. We took a ferry to the statue on independence day.

   A ferry

   B statue

   C none

   D independence day

3. The statue was made in the 19th century by mr. bartholdi.

   A mr. bartholdi

   B century

   C mr.

   D none

4. He modeled the face on his mother's.

   A mother's

   B modeled

   C face

   D none

5. The statue's pedestal was made by mr. Hunt.

   A pedestal

   B statue's

   C none

   D mr.

6. This artwork was dedicated by our 22nd president.

   A dedicated

   B artwork

   C president

   D none

Review

✓ Rewrite correctly the words in each sentence that should have capital letters. If a sentence has no capitalization mistakes, write *C*.

1. Last summer my family visited some American monuments.

2. In july we went to the Gateway Arch in St. Louis.

3. It was designed by mr. eero Saarinen.

4. In august we visited Mount Rushmore in South Dakota.

5. A ceremony is held there each summer night from monday through sunday.

6. On a saturday in september we saw a monument in New York.

7. It was the tomb of general Grant.

8. My grandma said the memorial honors mrs. grant also.

✓ Write the sentences. Use capital letters correctly.

9. In april, we saw a memorial for president franklin delano roosevelt, our 32nd president.

10. I went with aunt janet to the memorial.

11. On tuesday we saw sculptures of the president.

12. On wednesday we learned more about mrs. Roosevelt.

13. My aunt and uncle saw the memorial on veterans day.

14. Roosevelt was born on january 30, 1882.

15. The memorial was dedicated may 2, 1997.

16. In june, uncle ed will take me to the Jefferson Memorial.

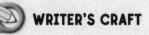

WRITER'S CRAFT

Paraphrasing

When you take notes on facts in a book or article, you **paraphrase** the article. Use these tips.

- Paraphrase only the main ideas, not unimportant details. Make sure you paraphrase the facts correctly.
- Use your own words, not those of the author.
- Copy especially interesting sentences in quotation marks.

Read the paragraph and each paraphrase of the paragraph. Write the best description from the box for each paraphrase.

Includes main ideas	Omits important information

The Liberty Bell is a symbol of American freedom. It was made in England and sent to Philadelphia. It cracked on its first ring and was repaired. On July 8, 1776, the bell was rung in honor of adopting the Declaration of Independence. Today the bell can be seen in Liberty Bell Pavilion in Philadelphia.

1. The Liberty Bell was made in England. It got cracked, but Americans fixed it.

2. The Liberty Bell stands for freedom to Americans because it was rung in 1776 when the Declaration of Independence was adopted. The Liberty Bell is still displayed in Philadelphia.

Taking Notes

> When you **take notes,** write the most important facts in an article. Try to put ideas into your own words. Put any phrases that you pick up word for word in quotation marks.

Notes are written in list form.

Writer uses abbreviations and does not always use complete sentences.

Writer uses quotation marks to show phrase is a direct quote from the original text.

Notes on "The Story of the Statue of Liberty"

Americans forgot about the S of L.

No money to finish the base

N.Y. newspaper asked public for money, and
   statue was finished.

Celebration—speeches, songs, speech by
   Pres. Cleveland—in 1886 when statue was
   in place. Bartholdi uncovered
   statue's face.

People coming on ships to live
in America first see S of L.

Fireworks above S of L
   part of July 4th celebration
   each year

"a truly unforgettable sight"

Abbreviations

An **abbreviation** is a shortened form of a word. Many abbreviations begin with a capital letter and end with a period.

- Some titles used for names of people are abbreviations. For example, *Dr.* is the abbreviation for *Doctor.* The title *Miss* is not abbreviated.

  Mr. Mark Elton Lewis   Ms. Susan Wang
  Mrs. Mendes

- An **initial** is the first letter of a name. It is written with a capital letter and is followed by a period.

  Mr. Mark E. Lewis   S. B. Wang   C. M. Mendes

- The names of days and months can be abbreviated. *May, June,* and *July* are not abbreviated.

Days of the Week
Sun. Mon. Tues. Wed. Thurs. Fri. Sat.
Months of the Year
Jan. Feb. Mar. Apr. Aug. Sept. Oct. Nov. Dec.

A Write each abbreviation. Be sure to capitalize letters and use periods correctly. If a phrase is correct, write *C.*

1. ms. Janine Lee
2. jan 24
3. Dr N D Bond
4. thurs, aug 2

5. B. C. Pepper
6. Mon., Dec. 13
7. mrs M A Dixon
8. tues, oct 8

B Some abbreviations can be used in sentences. Write the sentences. Write the abbreviations and initials correctly.

1. Mr G t Bryant has several birds.

2. He takes them to an animal doctor, dr E Rodriguez.

3. His son P J helps care for the family's birds.

4. The Bryants bought a bright yellow canary from ms Gray's pet store.

5. They named it Archie, after their friend Archibald p McNabb.

6. One day mrs Bryant noticed that Archie had stopped singing.

7. Neither dr. Rodriguez nor her assistant ms r m Lee knew what was wrong.

8. They talked with Gen F X Loomis, an army bird specialist.

9. "Maybe he needs friends," gen Loomis said.

10. The next day mr Bryant bought two more canaries from ms Gray.

C The following items are notes for a report. Rewrite each note. Use abbreviations and initials correctly for titles, names, days, and months whenever possible.

11. Mister Roger Tory Peterson, bird lover, born Friday, August 28, 1908

12. Roger Tory Peterson, member of National Audubon Society, named for John James Audubon

13. Mister Peterson wrote *A Field Guide to the Birds,* 1934

14. Roger Tory Peterson died Sunday, July 28, 1996

Test Preparation

 Write the letter of the correct abbreviation for each word or group of words.

1. December

  A dec

  B Dec

  C Decem

  D Dec.

2. Wednesday

  A Wed

  B Wed.

  C wed

  D wednes.

3. Doctor Ray

  A dr Ray

  B Dr Ray

  C Dr. Ray

  D dr. Ray

4. February

  A Feb

  B feb

  C feb.

  D Feb.

5. Monday, March 2

  A Mon, March 2

  B Mon., Mar. 2

  C Mon., mar. 2

  D mon., march 2

6. Mister King

  A Mr. King

  B mr King

  C Mr King

  D mr. King

Review

Write each name or date. Be sure to capitalize letters and use periods correctly. If a phrase is correct, write *C*.

1. Mrs Tanya Bright
2. Dr. Barbara A. Finch
3. Sun, aug 12
4. Mr and Mrs. J. T Adams
5. R. j. Moss
6. Thurs, sept. 1
7. Ms. Joan L. Rose
8. Tues., nov 13
9. Mr Carlton b Hayes
10. mon, oct. 30
11. miss h Elena Ruiz
12. Sat., Apr. 28

Some abbreviations can be used in sentences. Write the sentences. Write the abbreviations and initials correctly.

13. Our teacher, mr t n Frost, likes pet birds.
14. Dr Marian k Hardy told our class about parrots.
15. My neighbor, j g Jones, owns a rainbow-colored parrot from South America.
16. Mrs Sanchez said parakeets are related to parrots.
17. "Where do parakeets come from?" asked ms Torres.
18. dr. Hardy said they live in many warm places around the world.
19. My friend k v said they used to live in Florida.
20. That white cockatoo with a yellow crest belongs to mr and mrs Frost.
21. "A cockatoo is a kind of parrot," said mrs Sanchez.
22. Mrs Sanchez, ms Torres, dr Hardy, and mr Frost are experts on parrots.

Including Important Details

When you write a research report, use the facts in your outline. Keep your topic, audience, and purpose in mind. Then **include the important details** about your topic.

The information below is part of an outline on the hua mei bird. The paragraph that follows it adds unimportant details to the information in the outline. Copy the sentences that have unimportant details.

> **B.** Appearance
>   **1.** 4–5 in. long
>   **2.** Grayish-yellow with black speckles
>   **3.** White marks above eyes
> **C.** Special Features
>   **1.** Fighting birds
>   **2.** Can be taught to sing
>   **3.** Name means "painted eyebrows"

The hua mei bird is 4 or 5 inches long. Canaries are much more colorful than this bird. It has unusual white marks above its eyes. These marks led to the bird's name, which is Chinese for "painted eyebrows." The hua mei is a fighting bird. I prefer peaceful birds. People have taught the hua mei bird to sing. Its melody is probably beautiful.

Write sentences about parrots based on the following details: 3 inches to 3 ft. long; brightly colored; thick, hooked bill.

Outlining

An **outline** organizes information about a topic. Before writing a research report, use your notes to make an outline.

- For most outlines, use words and phrases, not complete sentences. You may use abbreviations.
- Use Roman numerals for the main topics.
- Use capital letters for subtopics.
- Use numbers for details about the subtopics.

Title tells topic of outline. ——

There is no *A* unless there is a *B*, no *1* unless there is a *2*. Details about native homes are included with subtopic.

Every topic, subtopic, and detail begins with capital letter.

Popular Pet Birds

I. Parrots
  A. Native Homes: warm, tropical areas
  B. Appearance
    1. 3 in. to 3 ft. long
    2. Brightly colored
  C. Special Features
    1. Noisy, sociable
    2. Can learn to talk
II. Hua Mei
  A. Native Homes: forests of So. China
  B. Appearance
    1. 4–5 in. long
    2. White marks above eyes
  C. Special Features
    1. Fighting birds
    2. Can be taught to sing
    3. Name means "painted eyebrows"

Combining Sentences

When you **combine sentences,** you join two sentences that are about the same topic. You make them into one sentence.

- You can join two simple sentences to form a compound sentence. Add a comma and a conjunction such as *and, but,* or *or.*

  We saw a mural. Its bright colors amazed us.
  We saw a mural, and its bright colors amazed us.

- You can combine two sentences that have the same subject.

  The mural was in a cave. The mural seemed very old.
  The mural was in a cave and seemed very old.

- You can combine two sentences that have the same predicate.

  Michael liked the mural. I liked the mural.
  Michael and I liked the mural.

A Combine each pair of short sentences into a compound sentence. Use a comma and the conjunction in ( ).

1. People in France explored caves. They found murals. (and)

2. Were the murals painted by modern people? Were they painted by cave people long ago? (or)

3. The murals showed animals from long ago. The art style dates back thousands of years. (and)

4. People can view the cave murals. They must be careful. (but)

B Combine each pair of sentences with a conjunction that works. Use the underlined words only once in your new sentence. Do not use commas in your sentences.

1. <u>Our teacher</u> saw an empty wall downtown. <u>Our teacher</u> got permission to paint a mural on it.

2. <u>We</u> drew pictures on the wall. <u>We</u> painted them with bright colors.

3. Our teacher <u>worked every day for weeks</u>. The students <u>worked every day for weeks</u>.

4. Dancers <u>are pictured on the mural</u>. Musicians <u>are pictured on the mural</u>.

5. Our parents <u>came to see the mural</u>. Friends <u>came to see the mural</u>.

6. <u>Making a mural is</u> fun. <u>Making a mural is</u> difficult.

7. <u>We could</u> make a mural next year. <u>We could</u> choose another kind of art.

C Combine the items in each pair. Combine subjects or predicates, or write compound sentences. Use a conjunction that works. Remember to use commas in compound sentences.

8. Robert draws well. Some other students draw even better.

9. Robert might become a cartoonist. He might illustrate children's books.

10. Sadie likes pastels. She doesn't like watercolors.

11. Yolanda wants to be a sculptor. Michael wants to be a photographer.

12. The students work hard. They have fun as well.

Test Preparation

 Write the letter of the words that complete the sentence correctly.

1. Jon likes ___ prefers music.

   A art, But Toby

   B art or Toby

   C art, but Toby

   D art and Toby

2. You can go to the ___ the concert.

   A museum, or

   B museum but

   C museum, and

   D museum or

3. I saw a ___ saw a collage.

   A mural and Andy

   B mural or Andy

   C mural, or Andy

   D mural, and Andy

4. This picture is ___ is larger.

   A huge but that one

   B huge and that one

   C huge, but that one

   D huge, or that one

5. I will look at ___ paintings.

   A sculptures but

   B sculptures, and

   C sculptures and

   D sculptures, or

6. You can get into ___ must wait in line.

   A this show but you

   B this show, but you

   C this show, and you

   D this show and you

Review

✓ Combine each pair of short sentences into a compound sentence. Use a comma and the conjunction in ( ).

1. Paintings are popular. There are many other kinds of art. (but)

2. Collages combine different items. Murals include many small pictures. (and)

3. Some sculptors use marble. Others use metals. (and)

4. Potters shape clay with their hands. They use a potter's wheel. (or)

5. Will you make a vase? Would you rather shape a pot? (or)

6. Enjoy the paintings at the museum. Don't forget the other art. (but)

✓ Combine each pair of sentences with a conjunction that works. Use the underlined words only once in your new sentence.

7. <u>I</u> like to go to the museum. <u>I</u> look at my favorite pictures.

8. <u>My favorite painting</u> is set in the desert. <u>My favorite painting</u> shows an old barn.

9. Henri Matisse <u>painted still lifes</u>. Claude Monet <u>painted still lifes</u>.

10. <u>Vincent Van Gogh</u> painted sunflowers. <u>Vincent Van Gogh</u> also drew a starry sky.

11. <u>Van Gogh's work is</u> beautiful. <u>Van Gogh's work is</u> strange.

12. <u>I could become</u> a painter. <u>I could become</u> a sculptor.

Topic Sentences

A **topic sentence** tells the main idea of
a paragraph. The topic sentence is often
the first sentence of a paragraph that gives
information.

 Read the three topic sentences. Write the sentence that
would be the best topic sentence for each group of details.

Topic Sentences

Many artists have painted murals.
Murals are not hard to make.
You can see murals in many different places.

1. Put a big piece of white paper on a bulletin board.
Decide on a topic such as school sports. Have each
person paint one scene for the mural.

2. Some murals are painted on skyscrapers near city
highways. Others are painted in neighborhood parks
or inside public buildings.

3. People who lived in caves long ago painted murals.
An Italian artist, Michelangelo, painted a famous
mural on a ceiling in the 1500s. Many Americans
painted murals in the 1960s.

Write a topic sentence for the following details.

Some murals show important people. Others show
beautiful places. Still others show events from history.

Informational Paragraph

An **informational paragraph** gives facts on a topic. It usually begins with a topic sentence that tells the main idea of the paragraph. The other sentences in the paragraph give details that support the main idea. A concluding sentence sums up the paragraph.

Topic sentence gets readers' interest and tells paragraph's main idea.

Other sentences give facts about main idea.

Conclusion sums up paragraph's main idea.

Large Art

What is big and bright and enjoyed by many people? A mural is an art form that has all these traits. A mural is a painting on a large surface such as a wall, either inside or outside. The pictures on a mural tell a story. A mural may show events in history, such as the history of Native Americans. It may show famous people, such as jazz musicians. The bright colors and vivid styles of murals attract everyone's attention. Many famous artists have painted murals. People like you and me can paint murals too. Murals are artworks for everyone.

Commas

Use a **comma** and a conjunction to join two sentences.

I went outside, and I saw some ants.

Use **commas** to separate words in a series.

The ants were small, brown, and very active.

Use a **comma** after the greeting and the closing of a friendly letter.

Dear Ellie,   Your friend,

Use a **comma** between the name of a city and a state in an address.

Casper, WY 82602   Cleveland, Ohio

Use a **comma** to separate the month and day from the year.

April 28, 2007

A Write *C* if commas are used correctly in the sentence. Write *NC* if commas are not used correctly.

1. Ants are social insects, and they live in groups called colonies.

2. Ants may live in rotten logs leaves or thorns.

3. I finished my report on ants on October 3, 2007.

4. An ant's sting is painful but it isn't poisonous.

5. That scientist lives in Miami, Florida.

B Write each line of the letter. Add commas where they are needed.

1. Dear Caroline

2. Frankie and I went to the park and we took a picnic lunch.

3. On our picnic we had sandwiches pickles and fruit.

4. It was summer and the day was very hot.

5. Coming toward us was a line of big ants little ants and medium ants.

6. Frankie said there are many ants in Tulsa Oklahoma.

7. We moved our food and Frankie left stale bread on the table.

8. Soon red ants brown ants and black ants were eating the bread.

9. The date of our victory over the ants was August 15 2006.

10. Your friend
    Eliza

C Answer each question with a complete sentence. Make your writing clear by using commas correctly.

11. What are three of your favorite hobbies?

12. What was the month, date, and year when you turned 6?

13. What is the name of the city and state or city and country where you were born?

14. What two subjects do you enjoy most at school? Write a compound sentence for your answer.

15. Do you like ants? Write a compound sentence for your answer.

Test Preparation

Write the letter of the words that complete the sentence correctly.

1. Dear ____

  A Cousin Peter

  B Cousin, Peter,

  C Cousin Peter,

  D Cousin, Peter

2. We went on a hike on ____.

  A April 23 2007

  B April, 23, 2007

  C April 23. 2007

  D April 23, 2007

3. Our hike took place near ____.

  A Albany, New York

  B Albany New York

  C Albany, New, York

  D Albany New, York

4. We hiked in the ____ many insects.

  A woods and we saw

  B woods, and we saw

  C woods, And we saw

  D woods or we saw

5. We saw ____.

  A beetles crickets and ants

  B beetles crickets, and, ants

  C beetles, crickets and, ants

  D beetles, crickets, and ants

6. Your ____

  A favorite cousin, Tad

  B favorite, cousin, Tad

  C favorite cousin, Tad,

  D favorite, cousin, Tad

Review

Write *C* if commas are used correctly in the sentence. Write *NC* if commas are missing or are not used correctly.

1. My dad studies insects and he loves his work.
2. He has studied insects in Hawaii Brazil, and Costa Rica.
3. He saw enormous butterflies near San Jose, Costa Rica.
4. Dad went to Africa on July 4 2003.
5. There he saw huge moths ants and mosquitoes.
6. One day we went to the park, and Dad showed me some grasshoppers.
7. There are a million different insects and Dad wants to study them all.

Write each sentence. Add commas where they are needed.

8. Some insects are helpful and some are harmful.
9. Bees make honey and silkworms create silk.
10. Ladybugs are harmless but they eat many harmful insects.
11. Fleas flies and mosquitoes can carry diseases.
12. Moths eat cloth and termites eat wood.
13. Locusts weevils and some beetles eat crops.
14. Did you hear this prediction from a scientist in Paris France?
15. She said the world will be overrun by insects by January 1 3000.
16. If insects come, I would prefer to be in Juneau Alaska.

Elaborating

When you **elaborate,** you write details to support your main idea. Use specific words to show what you are describing. Replace words and phrases such as *things* and *a lot of* with specific words.

No   Those ants carried a lot of things.
Yes   Those ants carried hundreds of cake crumbs.

Choose words from the box to replace the underlined word or words in each sentence. Write the new sentence.

> like a weightlifter picking up a huge barbell
> books and magazine articles
> sugar crystals many times their weight
> a huge bread crumb
> ten times its size

1. Once I saw an ant carrying <u>something</u>.

2. The bread crumb was <u>very big</u>.

3. Ants can lift <u>heavy things</u>.

4. This is <u>neat</u>.

5. I want to read <u>a lot of stuff</u> about ants.

Elaborate on the following topic sentence by writing two details. Use specific words.

Ants come in many different colors and sizes.

Writing About a Picture

When you **write about a picture,** you describe the picture's details. You may explain why you think the picture is especially interesting, beautiful, or creative.

Topic sentence gets readers' interest and describes picture.

Next sentences use vivid descriptive words to elaborate on picture's traits.

Conclusion sums up why the picture is interesting.

A Big World

Huge creatures with antennae and six legs march through a dark forest covered with rocks and gravel. But wait! The huge creatures are really tiny ants. The forest is really blades of grass. The rocks and gravel are tiny grains of sand and dirt. This is a picture in *Two Bad Ants,* and it shows how big the world must look to ants. The picture shows a line of black ants marching along a white path. The ants are drawn in correct proportion to the grass. Yet people never see the ground and the grass from the ants' point of view. This picture gives people a whole new view of the world.

Quotations

Quotation marks (" ") show the exact words of a speaker.

- Use a comma to separate the speaker's exact words from the rest of the sentence.
- Capitalize the first word inside the quotation marks.
- Put the punctuation mark that ends the quotation inside the quotation marks.

> "I want to be a glassblower," said Elena.
>
> "Is that a hard job?" I asked.
>
> She replied, "You need good lungs!"

Quotation marks also indicate titles of short works, such as songs, poems, and stories.

> Elena sang "Burro Serenade."

A Write *C* if a sentence is correct. If it is not correct, make the corrections that are needed.

1. There are many ways to make glass into objects," Al said.

2. You can blow the hot glass with a blowpipe, Kit said.

3. Taylor mentioned, "you can press the glass into a mold.

4. Kevin added, "You can pour hot glass into a mold."

5. "You can make so many useful things with glass!" Sara exclaimed.

6. I asked, "Are some lamps made of glass?

B Write the sentences. Add capital letters, quotation marks, commas, and other punctuation marks as needed.

1. I read an article about the desert Rosanna said.

2. The title of the article was Not Always Hot and Dry.

3. At night deserts can get very cold Russell explained.

4. Olivia asked aren't deserts different in different places

5. Yes, some deserts are in cold climates replied Ms. Lacy.

6. Manuel said, I lived near the desert in Arizona.

7. It was really hot in summer he exclaimed.

8. Manuel wrote a poem called Song of the Desert.

9. What was it like in spring Anna asked.

10. In spring it rained, and wildflowers grew Manuel replied.

C Answer each question with a complete sentence. Make each answer a quotation followed by the words *I said*. Use quotation marks and other punctuation correctly.

Example Do you like to travel?
"Yes, I like to travel," I said.

11. Do you like the desert, mountains, beach, or another natural place best?

12. What is your favorite part of this place?

13. What would you do in this place if you took a trip there?

14. What animals would you see in this place?

15. What would you take on your trip?

Test Preparation

✓ Write the letter of the choice that correctly completes the sentence.

1. "I can play the ____

   A flute, Ross said.

   B flute," Ross said.

   C flute, Ross said."

   D flute" Ross said.

2. Tara asked, "What kind of music ____

   A do you play.

   B do you play?

   C do you play"?

   D do you play?"

3. ____ like lively songs."

   A Ross said, "I

   B Ross said, I

   C "Ross said, I

   D Ross said "I

4. "She has a wonderful ____

   A teacher, Tara exclaimed!"

   B teacher!" Tara exclaimed.

   C teacher! Tara exclaimed.

   D teacher." Tara exclaimed.

5. ____ songs do you like?"

   A Ross asked. "What

   B Ross asked, What

   C Ross asked, "What

   D Ross asked "What

6. ____ is Ross's favorite.

   A "Tomorrow

   B "Tomorrow"

   C "Tomorrow"

   D Tomorrow"

Review

✓ Write *C* if a sentence is correct. If it is not correct, make the corrections that are needed.

1. The class read a story called The Island Journey.

2. Can we go on a trip?" Pablo asked.

3. How about an imaginary trip? Ms. Adams replied.

4. Chris asked, "How do we do that?"

5. Ms. Adams said, "think about a place you want to go.

6. I'm thinking about a beautiful island, Danny said.

7. "The water is bright blue, Sophia said.

8. Green parrots are talking in the trees, Clifford said.

9. Ms. Adams exclaimed, "You're taking your trip already!"

✓ Write the sentences. Add capital letters, quotation marks, commas, and other punctuation marks as needed.

10. I went on a trip Ross said.

11. Sam asked where did you go?

12. I went to the bottom of the ocean Ross replied.

13. I saw purple fish and orange seahorses he said.

14. Amber said I went to the top of a mountain.

15. Tyler asked what was your favorite part of the trip

16. I could see the world for miles around Amber replied.

17. Tyler said I went to the desert at night.

18. I saw animals' eyes gleaming in the dark, he whispered.

Strong Conclusions

A **strong conclusion** sums up the main idea of a paragraph in a vivid way.

Read each paragraph and its possible conclusions. Write the letter of the most effective conclusion for the paragraph.

1. A mountaintop looks beautiful from far away, but it is a harsh place for people who visit. The higher you go, the worse the weather gets. At the top of a high mountain, snow swirls in a stiff wind. Temperatures are below freezing. ____

A Mountains are very beautiful.

B So everyone should climb mountains.

C Unless you are an experienced mountain climber, the best way to enjoy a tall mountain is from the ground.

2. The rain forest is a noisy and colorful part of the natural world. Monkeys screech, frogs croak, and insects chirp. The plants create a lush green world that contrasts with the brilliant reds and yellows of flowers and birds. ____

A A rain forest has more sights and sounds than the most exciting adventure movie.

B Some of the animals that you see in rain forests include monkeys and frogs.

C You should avoid the rain forest altogether if you have certain kinds of allergies.

Writing Good Paragraphs

A **good paragraph** has a topic sentence that tells the paragraph's main idea. It has supporting details that tell more about the main idea and are organized in a logical way. A good paragraph ends with a strong conclusion.

Topic sentence gets readers' interest and states paragraph's main idea.

Next six sentences provide supporting details. They are arranged in two groups: plants and animals.

Conclusion vividly sums up paragraph's main idea.

Life in the Desert

The desert seems like a hot, empty place, but it is really full of life. Deserts are very dry as well as hot, but plants that need little water grow there. These include cactuses, grasses, and even some trees. When it does rain, wildflowers and green plants bloom. Many animals like the dry, hot desert climate. Snakes and lizards live under rocks during the day. Larger animals such as foxes and jackrabbits may also spend time in the desert.

When you think of a desert, you may think of a dead brown landscape. However, you will find that nature has amazing variety there.

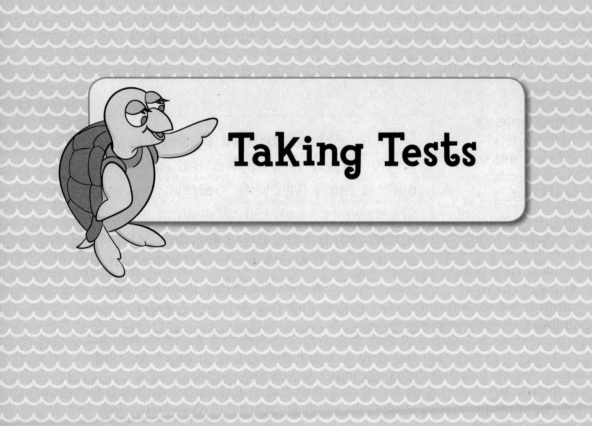

Taking Tests

Follow these tips when writing for a test:

Before Writing

- Read the prompt carefully. What does it ask you to do?
- Write down key words that name your audience *(warn <u>people who eat junk food</u>)*, state the purpose of the composition *(<u>give directions</u>)*, and tell you how to organize your points *(provide <u>step-by-step instructions</u>)*.
- Use a graphic organizer to plan your composition.
- Determine the tone of your writing (friendly, formal).

During Writing

- Reread the prompt as you write to make sure you are on topic.
- Keep in mind your graphic organizer and stay focused.
- Write a good beginning. You might engage readers with a thought-provoking question or an interesting fact.
- Develop and elaborate ideas. Support your main idea, your observations, or your opinion.
- Write a strong ending. Try to write a "clincher" sentence to provide a clear ending. You might add a final comment of your own or challenge your reader with a command.

After Writing

- Check your grammar and mechanics (punctuation, spelling).
- Reread the prompt and review your work. There's still time to add words or correct errors.

Writing a Personal Narrative

A **test** may ask you to write a personal narrative. Your narrative needs to have a beginning, middle, and end. Use time-order words such as *then* and *after*. Follow the tips below.

Understand the prompt. Make sure you know what to do. Read the prompt. A prompt for a personal narrative could look like this:

> Write a personal narrative about an experience that made you feel proud of yourself. Be sure to choose just one experience or event for your narrative.

Key phrases are *personal narrative, proud of yourself,* and *one experience or event.*

Find a good topic. Choose an important event that you remember well. Think about the details you want to include.

Organize your ideas. Make a story organizer like this:

Event   I earned money to buy a new bike.

When?   Last summer

Why?   I outgrew my bike.

   1. I needed a new bike and saw one I wanted.

   2. I handed out flyers about jobs I could do.

   3. I did jobs and earned money.

   4. I bought the bike.

Write a good beginning. An exciting topic sentence will make your audience want to read more.

Develop and elaborate ideas. Use information from your story organizer. Include words that show time.

Write a strong ending. The end of your personal narrative can be exciting.

Check your work. Reread and make any changes.

See how the personal narrative below answers the prompt and has a clear beginning, middle, and end.

1 — My bike and I had changed over the past two years. I was much bigger. My bike was scratched and dented. This spring it was time to take action. I saw a bright red mountain — 4
bike at the Big Wheel. It was the bike for me!
2 — To earn money for the bike, I passed out a flyer listing the jobs I could do. Soon neighbors were calling me to mow grass and wash cars. — 3
By July, I had saved enough money. I was so proud of myself. Now I ride every day. If you
5 — see a blur on the bike path, that's me!

1. The opening sentence grabs the reader's attention.

2. Time-order words show the sequence of events.

3. Exclamatory sentences add interest.

4. Vivid details help readers picture the scene.

5. The strong ending shows the writer's personality.

Writing a How-to Report

A **test** may ask you to write a how-to report. Remember to include all the steps. Use words such as *first* and *next* to help order the steps. Follow the tips below.

Understand the prompt.   Read the prompt carefully. A prompt for a how-to report could look like this:

> Write a report that gives steps on how to make or do something. Make your report interesting and easy to understand. Explain all the steps and materials needed.

Key words and phrases are *steps*, *how to make or do something*, and *materials*.

Find a good topic.   Choose an activity you can do well.

Organize your ideas.   Create a how-to chart. Write the name of the task, the materials needed, an introduction, a list of steps, and an ending. A list of steps might look like the one below:

Steps	Get pine cone, string, peanut butter, margarine, and birdseed.
	Tie the string to the pine cone.
	Mix peanut butter and margarine and spread on pine cone.
	Roll pine cone in birdseed.

Write a good beginning. Write a strong opening sentence that tells readers what you are about to explain.

Develop and elaborate ideas. Refer to your chart to help you organize ideas. Use precise nouns and order words.

Write a strong ending. Use the ending to summarize.

Check your work. Read and check your report.

See how the how-to report below answers the prompt.

1 —— Do you like to watch birds in your yard? Then make this easy bird feeder. You will need a pine cone, a long string, peanut butter, margarine, and birdseed.

First, tie the string to the top of the pine cone. Then make a mixture of half peanut butter and half margarine. Spread it all over the pine cone. Next put some birdseed on a plate. Roll the pine cone around so birdseed sticks all over it.

Finally, hang the pine cone on a tree in your yard. Now see how many birds live in your neighborhood!

2
3
4
5

1. The opening question grabs the reader's attention.

2. The writer uses words that show the order of steps.

3. Precise nouns make the explanation clear.

4. The steps are in an order that makes sense.

5. The ending sums up the explanation.

Writing a Compare/Contrast Essay

A **test** may ask you to write a compare/contrast essay. Use words that show likenesses (*and, also, both*) and differences (*although, while, but*). Follow the tips below.

Understand the prompt. Read the prompt carefully. A prompt for a compare/contrast essay could look like this:

Write an essay comparing and contrasting two things in nature, such as two seasons or two natural places. Show how they are alike and different.

A key phrase is *comparing and contrasting.*

Find a good topic. Choose two natural features that have many things in common as well as several differences.

Organize your ideas. Make a compare/contrast organizer. You can start with either likenesses or differences.

Main Idea Spring and fall, my favorite seasons, are different and alike.			
Different		**Same**	
Spring	Fall	Spring	Fall
Growth begins	Growth ends	In-between	In-between
New plants	Dying plants	Bright colors	Bright colors
		Not hot or cold	Not hot or cold

Write a good beginning. Draw your reader in.

Develop and elaborate ideas. Build on your organizer.

Write a strong ending. Sum up your ideas.

Check your work. Change what you want.

See how the essay below follows the prompt.

> **1** Spring and fall, my favorite seasons, are different and yet alike. **3** They are different because one is the time when growth starts, **2** but the other is when it ends. Spring has new green buds, while fall has dying leaves.
>
> Still, the seasons are alike in some ways. **2** First, both are in-between seasons. Neither is too cold or too warm. Both also have lovely **4** colors. Spring has bright flowers. Fall has red and orange leaves. Finally, both spring and fall lead to more extreme seasons. Fall leads to cold winter. Spring leads to hot summer. But fall and spring are not too hot or too cold. **5** They're both just right!

1. The first sentence introduces the main idea.

2. Words for likenesses and differences make ideas clear.

3. The comparison and contrast points are clear.

4. Vivid word choice helps readers picture the seasons.

5. The conclusion sums up why the seasons are the writer's favorites.

Writing a Story

> A **test** may ask you to write a story. You will need to think of a character and something that happens to him or her. Follow the tips below.

Understand the prompt. Make sure you know what to do. Read the prompt carefully. A prompt for a story could look like this:

> Write a story about a character and one event that happens. The event could be interesting, funny, or scary. Be sure your story has a beginning, middle, and ending.

Key words and phrases are *story*, *character*, *one event*, *beginning*, *middle*, and *ending*.

Find a good topic. Choose an interesting character and one specific thing that he or she does.

Organize your ideas. Make a story organizer.

Character Tim, who loves holidays

Setting Tim's house

Event Tim learns about a new holiday.

   1. Tim's friend Lee comes to visit, wearing dragon costume.

   2. Tim asks about the costume.

   3. Lee tells Tim about Chinese New Year.

   4. Tim plans to celebrate Chinese New Year too.

Write a good beginning. An interesting opening sentence will make your reader eager to read on.

Develop and elaborate ideas. Use information from your story organizer.

Write a strong ending. Show how your character changes.

Check your work. Reread your work carefully. Make needed changes.

See how the story below follows the prompt.

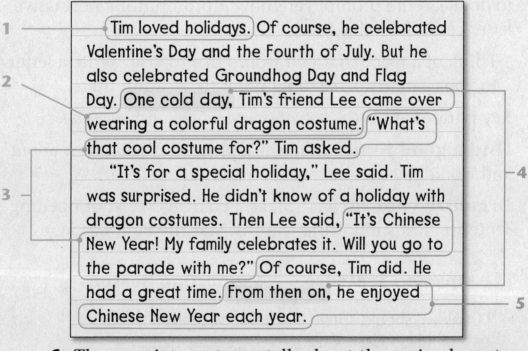

1 — Tim loved holidays. Of course, he celebrated Valentine's Day and the Fourth of July. But he also celebrated Groundhog Day and Flag Day.

2 — One cold day, Tim's friend Lee came over wearing a colorful dragon costume. "What's that cool costume for?" Tim asked.

3 —
4 —

"It's for a special holiday," Lee said. Tim was surprised. He didn't know of a holiday with dragon costumes. Then Lee said, "It's Chinese New Year! My family celebrates it. Will you go to the parade with me?" Of course, Tim did. He had a great time. From then on, he enjoyed Chinese New Year each year.

5 —

1. The opening sentence tells about the main character.

2. The story event is introduced in the first paragraph.

3. Quotations add interest.

4. Time-order words show the sequence of events.

5. The ending tells how the event changes the main character.

Writing a Persuasive Letter

A **test** may ask you to write a persuasive letter. When you choose your topic, think of reasons that will convince your reader. Use words such as *should* and *most important*. Follow the tips below.

Understand the prompt. Make sure you know what to do. Read the prompt carefully. A prompt for a persuasive letter could look like this:

> Think of a place that you would like to visit. Write a letter to your parents persuading them to vacation there.

Key phrases are *letter*, *parents*, *persuading*, and *vacation*.

Find a good topic. Choose a place that you know about and would like to visit.

Organize your ideas. Make a chart. Write your opening sentence. List supporting reasons. Star the best reason.

Opening Sentence	Supporting Reasons
I think we should spend part of July in Cape Cod.	Relax as a family* Friend goes there Bay and ocean Wide, clean beaches Hotels and campgrounds

Write a good beginning. State your main reason for writing the letter in the first sentence.

Develop and elaborate ideas. Use the reasons from your chart. Use persuasive words and phrases.

Write a strong ending. Write a convincing ending.

Check your work. Make any corrections.

See how the letter below addresses the prompt.

Dear Mom and Dad:

1 — I think we should spend part of July in Cape Cod, Massachusetts. My best friend Ella

2 — stays there every summer. Ella says that the Cape has great hotels and safe campgrounds.

3 — We can swim in the bay and the ocean. Ella showed me pictures of the wide, clean beaches. Most important, on Cape Cod we — 4 could enjoy ourselves as a family. I hope that — 5 you will decide on Cape Cod for this year's safe and enjoyable family vacation.

Your daughter,

Tracy

1. The letter begins with the reason for writing.

2. Language is persuasive.

3. Reasons are clear and well-stated.

4. The most important reason comes last.

5. This ending makes a strong statement.

Writing a Summary

A **test** may ask you to write a summary from a graph, time line, or chart. You will need to read the information carefully and use it in your own sentences. Follow the tips below.

Organize your ideas.   You will need to decide how to present the facts. Think about which facts you want to use first and which you will save until the end.

Write a good beginning.   Get your reader's attention. Think of an opening sentence that presents the main idea.

Fact Sheet About the White House

Purpose
- Home for President and family

When it was built
- Begun in 1792, lived in by President Adams in 1800
- Burned by British in War of 1812, rebuilt by 1817

Building features
- Main building with curved porch
- West wing offices for President and staff, east wing for military aides

What tourists see
- Five rooms on first floor: State Dining Room, Red Room, Blue Room, Green Room, East Room

---

Develop and elaborate ideas. Include facts from your fact sheet that support your main idea.

Write a strong ending. Write sentences that pull the information together.

Check your work. Add any missing information.

See how the summary below uses the information.

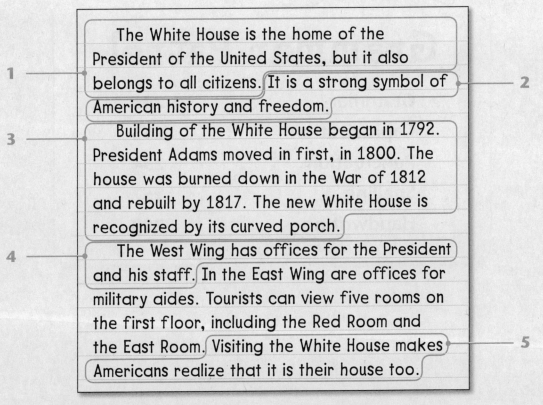

The White House is the home of the President of the United States, but it also belongs to all citizens. It is a strong symbol of American history and freedom.

Building of the White House began in 1792. President Adams moved in first, in 1800. The house was burned down in the War of 1812 and rebuilt by 1817. The new White House is recognized by its curved porch.

The West Wing has offices for the President and his staff. In the East Wing are offices for military aides. Tourists can view five rooms on the first floor, including the Red Room and the East Room. Visiting the White House makes Americans realize that it is their house too.

1. The opening sentence states the main idea.

2. The next sentence express the writer's feelings.

3. The history is explained in order.

4. Use a new paragraph when the topic changes.

5. The ending connects to the writer's main idea.

Grammar Patrol

Grammar Patrol

adjective   An adjective describes a noun or a pronoun.

> Ponds are *active* places.
> *Several* chipmunks run through the *wet* grass.

Adjectives have two different forms that are used to make comparisons.

- Use the *–er* form of an adjective to compare two persons, places, or things.

> Frogs have *smoother* skin than toads.

- Use the *–est* form of an adjective to compare three or more persons, places, or things.

> Snails are the *slowest* pond creatures.

- The words *more* and *most* are often used with adjectives of two or more syllables to make comparisons.

> The ducks were *more comical* than usual.
> The goose is the *most common* bird here.

- Some adjectives show comparison in a special way. The correct forms of *good*, *bad*, *much*, and *little* are shown below.

good weather	*better* weather	*best* weather
bad storm	*worse* storm	*worst* storm
much snow	*more* snow	*most* snow
little fog	*less* fog	*least* fog

article   The words, *a*, *an*, and *the* are a special kind of adjective. They are called articles. *The* is used with both singular and plural nouns. *A* and *an* are used only with singular nouns.

> *The* animals at *the* pond are very busy.
> *A* friend and I spent *an* afternoon there.

- Use *a* before a word that begins with a consonant sound.

> *a* beaver   *a* pleasant afternoon

- Use *an* before a word that begins with a vowel sound.

> *an* owl   *an* underwater plant

adverb   A word that describes a verb is an adverb.

- Some adverbs ask the question "How?"

   The fox hides *slyly* behind the bushes. (how?)

- Some adverbs answer the question "Where?"

   Aesop wrote fables *here*. (where?)

- Other adverbs answer the question "When?"

   Often a fable tells about one event. (when?)

Adverbs can be used to compare actions.

- Use the *–er* form or *more* to compare two actions. Most adverbs that end in *–ly* use *more*.

   The ant worked *harder* than the cricket.
   The tortoise moved *more steadily* than the hare.

- Use the *–est* form or *most* to compare three or more actions. Most adverbs that end in *–ly* use *most*.

   The ant worked *hardest* of all the insects.
   The tortoise moved *most steadily* of all.

The word *not* is an adverb. It means "no." Do not use two words that mean "no" in the same sentence.

   Wrong: It *wouldn't never* matter to me.
   Right: It *wouldn't* ever matter to me.
   Right: It would *never* matter to me.

contraction   A contraction is a shortened form of two words. An apostrophe replaces a letter or letters.

- Some contractions join a pronoun and a verb.

   I have never been in a dairy shed before.
   I've never been in a dairy shed before.

- Some contractions are formed from a verb and the word *not*.

   I *cannot* believe you *did not* bring your banjo.
   I *can't* believe you *didn't* bring your banjo.

noun   A noun names a person, place, or thing.

    The *settlers* came to *America* on a *ship*.
    (person)   (place)   (thing)

A **singular noun** names one person, place, or thing.

    The *settler* kept the *cow* in the *barn*.

A **plural noun** names more than one person, place, or thing.

    The *settlers* kept their *cows* in their *barns*.

- Add *-s* to form the plural of most nouns.

    colonist*s*   river*s*   pea*s*   chicken*s*

- Add *-es* to form the plural of nouns that end in *ch*, *sh*, *s*, *ss*, *x*, or *z*.

    bench*es*   bush*es*   bus*es*   box*es*

- If a noun ends in a consonant and *y*, change *y* to *i* and add *-es* to form the plural.

    Singular: library   city   cherry
    Plural: librar*ies*   cit*ies*   cherr*ies*

- Some plurals are formed by changing the spelling of the singular noun.

    Singular: man   child   foot   mouse
    Plural: men   child*ren*   f*ee*t   m*ice*

- A few nouns have the same singular and plural forms.

    Singular: elk   moose   deer   sheep
    Plural: elk   moose   deer   sheep

A **common noun** names any person, place, or thing.

    A *colonist* founded the *town*.

A **proper noun** names a particular person, place, or thing.

    William Penn founded *Philadelphia*.

A **possessive noun** shows ownership.

- To form the possessive of a singular noun, add an apostrophe and s ('s) to the singular noun.

    Ben Franklin's many talents amazed people.

- To form the possessive of a plural noun ending in s, add an apostrophe (s').

    shoemakers' hammers   *blacksmiths'* forges

- To form the possessive of a plural noun that does not end in s, add an apostrophe and s ('s).

    men's hats   *mice's* tails   two *deer's* tracks

preposition   A preposition is a word that shows how a noun or pronoun is related to other words in the same sentence.

    We sing *in* the car.

A preposition begins a group of words called a **prepositional phrase**. At the end of the phrase is a noun or pronoun called the **object of the preposition**.

    Preposition: The dog buried its bone *in* the yard.
    Prepositional phrase: *in the yard*
    Object of the proposition: *yard*

pronoun   A pronoun takes the place of a noun or nouns.

    Nouns: *Linda* writes *poems*.
    Pronouns: *She* enjoys writing *them*.

The pronouns *I, you, she, he, it, we,* and *they* are **subject pronouns**. Use these pronouns to replace nouns that are the subjects of sentences.

    Robert Frost had been a teacher and a farmer.
    He wrote many poems about nature.

The pronouns *me, you, him, her, it, us* and *them* are **object pronouns**. You can use these pronouns to replace nouns in the predicate of a sentence.

> Paul read *poems* to *Jill.*
> Paul read *them* to *her.*

The pronouns *my, your, his, her, its, our,* and *their* are **possessive pronouns**. A possessive pronoun shows ownership. Possessive pronouns can replace nouns.

> That *writer's* home is in the mountains.
> *Her* poems usually involve nature.

sentence   A sentence is a group of words that expresses a complete thought.

> *People of all ages enjoy hobbies.*

A **declarative sentence** makes a statement. It ends with a period (.).

> *Hobbies are important in people's lives.*

An **interrogative sentence** asks a question. It ends with a question mark (?).

> *What is your hobby?*

An **imperative** sentence gives a command or makes a request. It ends with a period (.).

> *Please get your kite ready.*   *Come to our party.*

An **exclamatory sentence** expresses strong feeling. It ends with an exclamation mark(!).

> *That kite will crash!*   *How happy I am!*

A **simple sentence** has one subject and one predicate. It expresses one complete thought.

> *Kites come in many different shapes.*

A **compound sentence** contains two simple sentences joined by the word *and, but,* or *or.* Use a comma in a compound sentence before the word *and, but,* or *or.*

> *The day was cool,* and *clouds drifted across the sun.*

subject and predicate The subject is the part of the sentence that names someone or something. The predicate tells what the subject is or does. Both the subject and the predicate may be one word or many words.

> *Currents/move ocean water around the world.*
> *The most common mineral/is salt.*
> *Ocean water/moves.*
> *Sea water/flows in vast streams.*

The **simple subject** is the main word in the complete subject.

> The five biggest *oceans* are really one huge ocean.

A sentence may have more than one simple subject. The word *and* may be used to join simple subjects, making a **compound subject**. The simple subjects share the same predicate.

> Spiny *crabs* and colorful *fish* scurry along the underwater reef.

The **simple predicate** is the main word or words in the complete predicate.

> Ocean waters *flow* in vast streams.

A sentence may have more than one simple predicate. The word *and* may be used to join simple predicates, making a **compound predicate**. The simple predicates share the same subject.

> Some worms *live* and *feed* in the ocean.

verb A verb is a word that shows action or being.

> Nina *paints* in art class. (action)
> That picture *is* beautiful. (being)

An **action verb** shows action. It tells what the subject of a sentence does.

> The art teacher *welcomed* the students.

A verb can be more than one word. The **main verb** is the most important verb. A **helping verb** works with the main verb.

> Many people have *admired* Picasso's paintings. (main verb)
> His name *is* known all over the world. (helping verb)

A **linking verb** shows being. It tells what the subject is or was.

> Grandma Moses *was* a famous artist.

When the correct subject and verb are used together, we say they agree. The form of the linking verb *be* that is used depends on the subject of the sentence. Study the following chart.

Using the Forms of *be*

Use *am* and *was*	with *I*
Use *is* and *was*	with *she, he, it,* and singular nouns
Use *are* and *were*	with *we, you, they,* and plural nouns

The **tense** of a verb shows the time of the action.

A verb in the **present tense** shows action that happens now.

> Eli *forms* the tiles.

A verb in the present tense must agree with the subject of the sentence.

- With *he, she, it,* or a singular noun, add *-s* or *-es* to the verb.
  > The student learn*s*.   My cousin teach*es*.   He walk*s*.

- If a verb ends in *ch, sh, s, ss, x,* or *z,* add *-es*. Notice the word *teaches* above.

- With *I, you, we, they,* or a plural noun, do not add *-s* or *-es*.
  > The students learn.   My cousins teach.   They walk.

A verb in the **future tense** shows action that will happen. The future tense is formed with the helping verb *will*.

> Ann *will create* a vase.

A verb in the **past tense** shows action that already happened.

Lee *washed* pots.

The past tenses of irregular verbs are not formed by adding *-ed*. Some irregular verbs are shown in the following chart.

Verb	Past	Past with *have, has,* or *had*
begin	began	begun
bring	brought	brought
come	came	come
do	did	done
eat	ate	eaten
fall	fell	fallen
find	found	found
fly	flew	flown
give	gave	given
go	went	gone
grow	grew	grown
ride	rode	ridden
run	ran	run
see	saw	seen
take	took	taken
throw	threw	thrown
write	wrote	written

The spelling of some verbs changes when *-es* or *-ed* is added.

- If a verb ends in a consonant and *y*, change the *y* to *i* before adding *-es* or *-ed*.

  study   stud*ies*   stud*ied*

- If a verb ends in one vowel and one consonant, double the final consonant before adding *-ed*.

  trap   tra*pped*   stir   sti*rred*

Capitalization

first word of a sentence   Every sentence begins with a capital letter.

> *People* enjoy having special projects.

proper noun   Each important word in a proper noun begins with a capital letter.

- Capitalize each word in the name of a person or pet.
  > *Patrice Gomez* owns a cat named *Duke*.

- Capitalize an initial in a name. Put a period after the initial.
  > William *L.* Chen is a doctor in our neighborhood.

- Capitalize a title before a name. If the title is an *abbreviation* (a shortened form of a word), put a period after it.
  > *President* Jefferson   *Dr.* Jonas Salk

- Capitalize every important word in the names of particular places or things.
  > *Statue of Liberty*   *Ellis Island*   *New York Harbor*

- Capitalize names of days, months, holidays, and special days.
  > *Tuesday*   *April*   *Fourth of July*

pronoun *I*   The pronoun *I* is always capitalized.

> May *I* go skating this afternoon?

letter   Capitalize the first word of the greeting and the first word of the closing of a letter.

> *Dear* Mother,   *Dear* Sir: *Sincerely* yours,

title of books, movies, songs, and other works   Capitalize the first word, the last word, and all of the important words in the title of works.

> The Secret Life of Harold the Bird Watcher
> "The Star-Spangled Banner"

quotation Begin the first word in a quotation with a capital letter.

> The Hare asked, *"How* about a race?"*

Punctuation

period Declarative sentences and imperative sentences end with a period (.).

> *I stood on the corner.*   *Wait for the signal.*

- Put a period after an initial in a name.

> J. P. Jones   Abigail S. Adams

- Put a period after an abbreviation (a shortened form of a word).

> *Mr.*   *Mrs.*   *Ms.*   *Dr.*

question mark An interrogative sentence ends with a question mark (?).

> *Do you have more than one hobby?*

exclamation mark An exclamatory sentence ends with an exclamation mark (!).

> *That kite will crash!*

comma A comma (,) is a signal that tells a reader to pause.

- Use a comma after *yes*, *no*, or *well* at the beginning of a sentence.

> *Yes*, I saw the display of Eskimo art.
> *Well*, my favorites were the bears made of silver.

- Use a comma to set off the name of the person spoken to.

> *Your painting is very beautiful, Roberta.*

- Use a comma to separate words in a series. A series is made up of three or more items. No comma is used after the last word in the series. The last comma goes before the word *and*.

> *The artists carve, smooth, and polish their work.*

- Use a comma to separate the city from the state.

    I grew up in *Tulsa, Oklahoma.*

- Use a comma to separate the day and the year.

    Pablo was born on *February 7, 2000.*

- Use a comma after the greeting of a friendly letter. Use a comma after the closing of a friendly or a business letter.

    Dear Kim,   *Your friend,*   *Yours truly,*

- Use a comma before the word *and, but,* or *or* in a compound sentence.

    The merchants crossed central Asia, and they reached China.

quotation marks   A quotation is the exact words someone speaks. Quotation marks (" ") show where a speaker's exact words begin and end.

- Use quotation marks before and after a quotation. Begin the first word in a quotation with a capital letter. When the quotation comes last, use a comma to separate the speaker from the quotation.

    The Tortoise said, "I'm not going to lose this race."

- When the quotation comes first, use a comma, a question mark, or an exclamation mark to separate the quotation from the speaker. The end mark of a quotation always comes just before the second quotation mark. Put a period at the end of the sentence.

    Statement: "Let's do something else," replied the Tortoise.
    Question: "Are you afraid you'll lose?" teased the Hare.
    Exclamation: "I'm not afraid!" snapped the Tortoise.

- Enclose the titles of stories, songs, poems, and articles in quotation marks.

    Story: "The Use of Force"
    Song: "Of Thee I Sing"
    Poem: "Dear March, Come In!"
    Article: "Let's Make Music"

Underline the titles of newspapers, magazines, books, plays, and movies.

In materials you read, these titles are printed in italics.

Newspaper: <u>Denver Post</u>
Magazine: <u>Popular Mechanics</u>
Book: <u>A Wind in the Door</u>
Play: <u>Man of La Mancha</u>
Movie: <u>Invaders from Mars</u>

apostrophe   Use an apostrophe (') to show where a letter or letters have been left out in a *contraction* (a shortened form of two words).

we'd (we + had)   *wasn't* (was + not)

• Use an apostrophe to form the possessive of a noun.

man's   *James's*   *men's*   *workers'*

colon   Use a colon (:) after the greeting in a business letter.

Dear Mr. Kurtz: *Dear Sir or Madam:*

Frequently Misspelled Words

a lot	everything	morning	then
afraid	except	myself	there
again	excited	of	they
almost	family	off	they're
already	favorite	once	thought
always	February	one	through
another	field	opened	to
are	finally	our	too
athlete	first	outside	took
basketball	found	people	tries
beautiful	friend	piece	truly
because	getting	presents	TV
before	government	pretty	two
believe	grabbed	probably	until
brother	happened	radio	upon
brought	heard	really	usually
buy	hero	right	vacation
caught	his	said	very
chocolate	hospital	scared	want
Christmas	house	school	was
clothes	I	separate	watch
control	I'm	should	weird
could	instead	since	we're
cousin	into	sincerely	were
Dad's	it's	something	what
decided	knew	sometimes	when
didn't	know	special	where
different	knowledge	started	which
disappear	let's	stopped	who
doesn't	library	successful	whole
don't	little	sure	with
enough	maybe	surprised	would
especially	might	swimming	you're
everybody	minute	that's	
everyone	Mom	their	

D'Nealian™ Alphabet

a b c d e f g h i

j k l m n o p q r s t

u v w x y z

A B C D E F G

H I J K L M N O

P Q R S T U V

W X Y Z . , ' ?

1 2 3 4 5 6

7 8 9 10

Manuscript Alphabet

a b c d e f g

h i j k l m n

o p q r s t u

v w x y z

A B C D E F G

H I J K L M N

O P Q R S T U

V W X Y Z , ' . ?

1 2 3 4 5 6

7 8 9 10

Cursive Alphabet

a b c d e f g

h i j k l m n

o p q r s t u

v w x y z

A B C D E F G

H I J K L M N

O P Q R S T U

V W X Y Z . , ' ?

1 2 3 4 5 6

7 8 9 10

Index

D

Dates. *See* Commas.
Describing words. *See* Adjectives.
Descriptive writing. *See* Writing.
Details, 2, 114, 162, 210

E

Evaluate own writing, 46–48
Exclamation mark, 68–71
Exclamations. *See* Sentences.
Expository writing. *See* Writing.

F

Focus/Ideas. *See* Writing.
Fragments. *See* Sentences.
Frequently misspelled words, 257

H

Handwriting, 258–260
Helping verbs. *See* Verbs.

I

Irregular verbs. *See* Verbs.
Items in series. *See* Commas.

J

Joining words. *See* Conjunctions.

L

Linking verbs. *See* Verbs.

M

Main idea, 2–3
Main verb. *See* Verbs.
Mechanics, 254–256
   apostrophe, 158–161
   comma, 194–197, 212–215, 218–221
   exclamation mark, 68–71
   period, 62–65, 68–71, 206–209
   question mark, 62–65
   quotation marks, 224–227

N

Narrative writing. *See* Writing.
Nouns, 247–248
   common, 80–83
   days of week, 80–83, 200–203
   holidays, 80–83, 200–203

months of year, 80–83,
200–203

plural, 86–89

  irregular, 92–95

possessive

  plural, 104–107

  singular, 98–101

proper, 80–83

singular, 86–89, 92–95,
98–101

states, 80–83

titles of people, 200–203,
206–209

O

Object of preposition,
164–167

Object pronouns. *See*
Pronouns.

Organization/Paragraphs.
See Writing.

P

Period, 62–65, 68–71, 206–209

Persuasive writing. *See*
Writing.

Phrases, 116–119, 164–167

Plural nouns. *See* Nouns.

Possessive nouns. *See* Nouns.

Predicates, 56–59, 250

  complete, 56–59

  compound, 212–215

Prepositional phrases,
164–167

Prepositions, 164–167, 248

Prompts, 26, 31, 36, 41, 79,
109, 139, 169, 232, 234, 236,
238, 240

Pronouns, 248–249

  object, 146–149

  plural, 140–143

  possessive, 152–155

  singular, 140–143

  subject, 146–149

Proofreading, 22–25

Proper nouns. *See* Nouns.

Punctuation, 50–53, 62–65,
68–71, 158–161, 194–197,
206–209, 212–215, 218–221,
224–227, 254–256 *See also*
Mechanics.

Purpose for writing, 2–3, 102

Q

Question mark, 62–65

Questions. *See* Sentences.